BRITISH FOREIGN POLICY
SINCE 1898

by

M. R. D. FOOT

LECTURER IN POLITICS,
KEBLE COLLEGE, OXFORD

LONDON

HUTCHINSON'S UNIVERSITY LIBRARY

Hutchinson's University Library
178–202 Great Portland Street, London, W.1

London   Melbourne   Sydney   Auckland
Bombay Johannesburg New York Toronto

First published 1956

Printed in Great Britain
by The Anchor Press, Ltd.,
Tiptree, Essex

CONTENTS

JX
1543
F6
1956

Nal 9D59

23NS9 Stechert (Hist)

5

CONTENTS

ACKNOWLEDGEMENTS

I am most grateful to the editor of this series, Sir Maurice Powicke; to Mr. H. G. Pitt of Worcester College; and to my wife. Each has gone through the first draft and much improved it. The faults that remain are my own.

Permission to republish extracts from works already in print is gratefully acknowledged to the following: Mrs. Neville Chamberlain, Professor Feiling, and Messrs. Macmillan (from *The Life of Neville Chamberlain*); Messrs. Chatto & Windus (from Wilfred Owen's 'Insensibility'); Sir Winston Churchill, and Odhams Press (from *The world crisis*) and Messrs. Cassell (from *The Second World War*); the Controller of Her Majesty's Stationery Office (from Gooch and Temperley *British Documents on the origins of the war*; Woodward, Butler, and Bury *Documents on British foreign policy*; the *Official report* of parliamentary debates; and several white papers); Sir Harold Nicolson (from *Curzon: the last phase*); Mr. Ezra Pound (for *Epitaph*, copyright 1926, 1952 by Ezra Pound and reprinted by permission of the publisher, *New Directions*); and to Professor Hugh and Mr. Christopher Seton-Watson and Messrs. Methuen (from R. W. Seton-Watson *From Munich to Danzig*).

I am also indebted to Miss M. Potter, of the School of Geography, Oxford, who drew the maps.

M. R. D. F.

Keble College,
Oxford.
4 August, 1956.

CHAPTER I

THE END OF 'SPLENDID ISOLATION'

1815–1898

'THERE is no such thing as a fixed policy,' Lord Salisbury wrote in 1896, 'because policy like all organic entities is always in the making.' The only fixed point which every British foreign policy has to start from is that the country lies on islands off the coast of Europe. Three other factors are of fundamental importance, but are always altering: the ambitions of other countries, the nature of British interests overseas, and the development of weapons of war. British governments can do much, of course, to affect these last two ; but during the British industrial revolution, and for long after, most state activity was mistrusted, and the expansion of foreign trade was left, as was the design of new weapons, to the unfettered discretion of individual entrepreneurs.

The secretary of state for foreign affairs—his office was founded in 1782—personally conducted the whole foreign policy of the country, with the agreement of the crown and of his cabinet colleagues on main lines of action ; he undertook responsibility before parliament for all that he did. For many years, not much interest was taken in overall foreign policy outside court and parliamentary circles. Yet lively public attention was devoted to the continent in the eighteen-fifties, and from the end of the seventies British voters were much interested, whether in enthusiasm or in censure, in the expansion of British power overseas. Most Britons were content with the belief, in which pride and boasting mingled, that they formed a race that was invincible ; and that their sure heroism would never be put to the test (unless they were sailors), because the navy could sink any foreign fleet, and so prevent any invasion.

Indeed, respect for British sea-power extended far outside Great Britain ; its predominance was taken for granted all the world over for ninety years or so after Trafalgar. The Monroe doctrine was announced from behind its guard ; the Spaniards, bowing to it, gave up their colonial claims in South America ; the

9

French never quite dared to challenge it; the Russians, when they found themselves at war with the British, prudently kept their battleships in harbour. It is doubtful whether the navy was in fact always as strong as it was thought to be; certainly towards the end of the century naval attention was devoted too much to paintwork and too little to proficiency. But what mattered was the legend of invincibility: everybody's policies for expansion overseas took this into account.

Plenty of room was left for manoeuvre within a framework that was broad as well as rigid. In the next few pages an attempt will be made to sketch out some of the main trends of nineteenth-century foreign policies, by way of introduction to the present study—a study of what happened when the fundamental postulates began to change, and Great Britain receded from the position in the very front rank she had regained under George III and maintained under Victoria.

When the great war against Napoleon ended in 1815 Great Britain, his only permanent opponent, took a leading part in arranging the peace settlement, through the person of the greatest of foreign secretaries, Lord Castlereagh. Practically single-handed, he secured a peace that was both magnanimous and lasting, that attained all the objects for which the British had fought, and that left five 'great powers', nicely balanced, to run the affairs of Europe. Castlereagh never sought popularity, and never was popular; but his judgement was exceptionally sound, and most of the criticisms aimed at his policies rest on false premises: many choices which seemed possible afterwards were not open to him at the time. For instance, he is particularly attacked for his neglect of nationalities, at a time when national feeling was immature, or even non-existent, in the areas concerned. Far from being the obedient tool of crafty continental reactionaries —another common charge against him—he acted with spirit and independence. Canning, who succeeded him when overwork drove him to suicide, was his disciple as well as his occasional rival; and imparted to British foreign policy the liberal tinge which distinguished it for half a century. The independence of the South American republics from Spain and Portugal, of Greece from Turkey, and of Belgium from Holland, all owed a considerable debt to British influence; and under the Canningite Lord Palmerston it came to be believed that British power would normally be exerted to protect new national states against old despotisms, if the new states inclined towards representative government as it was understood and respected in London. Palmerston's lifelong work to suppress the slave trade told in the same direction; and in his old age as prime minister, he was able to use the navy to hold the ring against possible interveners while Italian unity was achieved.

There were three blots on this British record of support for small nationalities. One was that hardly anyone in London was ready to admit Ireland's claim to national independence; and to profess abroad what was denied near at hand seemed, not unnaturally, hypocritical to many foreigners—including most Irishmen. Secondly, a desire to preserve Europe in balance inclined the British to support the already ailing power of Austria, and to disregard the nascent claims for autonomy of Austria's many subject races. And third, British support of smaller nations was not consistently followed through to the sticking point of war on their behalf; indeed, only for Greece did the British actually fight, and then allied with two strong powers against a weak one. In the cases of South America, of Belgium, and (in the end) of Italy, the threat that the British were ready to fight was enough to secure their aim; as it was in 1849, when they protected refugees at Constantinople from the Austro-Russian suppression of the Hungarian revolution (it was this incident that began thirty years of popular British enthusiasm for the Turks). But British strength was not always asserted with good judgement, or in causes of liberty. Greece in 1850, and Brazil in 1862, were shamefully bullied by the British fleet into paying unjust claims for damages.

On this matter of bullying, Palmerston ran into opposition from one of the most singular and most prescient statesmen of the time, Richard Cobden. Cobden, always pacific, was almost a pacifist—that is, he thought nearly all wars immoral; he and his friends conducted a vigorous propaganda in favour of arbitration and disarmament, on moral grounds. Outside a narrow circle of Quakers, they made few converts among the high-spirited English. But high spirits alone, as Palmerston found, do not guarantee success; it is not always easy to bully someone bigger than oneself. Their interests in the Levant led the British, allied with the French under their Emperor Napoleon III, to fight the Russians bravely, if incompetently, in the Crimean war; but they gave a much more sorry display in 1863. Having fallen out with Napoleon, they protested alone at Russia's oppression of the Poles, and were simply snubbed. Next winter Palmerston, then rising eighty, talked big about the integrity of Denmark, and had to act small when Bismarck invaded it. And Russia, at the time of Palmerston's death in 1865, remained a menace to Turkey, and indeed to the whole eastern Mediterranean.

The rise of Bismarck's Prussia to dominate central Europe posed a set of new problems for British statesmen; few of them knew him or Germany, and none of them understood either. All three of the main principles of Victorian foreign policy were called in question in the eighteen-sixties. Naval supremacy Bismarck, unlike Napoleon III, was too wise to challenge; but his career influenced another basic assumption in ways the British were slow to realize. It was not till the present century that it was seen that Prussian Germany had replaced France, the 'hereditary enemy', as the power most likely to dominate the continent and therefore most deserving (by standards then taken for granted) of British opposition; nor was it at first realized that the barrier erected with such care, at Vienna and in the Belgian settlement, to keep France from breaking into central Europe might now be needed to keep Germany from breaking out of it. And thirdly, the whole problem of the route to India, which the British were always vitally concerned to protect, needed thinking through again after the Suez canal was opened, by French enterprise, in 1869.

Disraeli, a brave and imaginative man, saw farther into the Suez tangle than most, and bought a large block of shares in the canal for the British government in 1875 (he bought 44% of the ordinary shares—not, as is often thought, a majority holding). But Disraeli's views on foreign affairs had been formed by Metternich after the old man had been hounded out of Vienna; and though Disraeli and Palmerston usually took opposite sides in home politics, and never sat in cabinet together, Disraeli showed a Palmerstonian *insouciance* and love of power —not backed by Palmerston's excellent command of detail based on hours of drudgery—when handling great power relations. He was lucky to avoid disaster at the end of the seventies, and was driven from office by the torrential force of Gladstone's eloquence in 1880. Gladstone opposed him on grounds of Christian principle, and convinced the electorate that Disraeli's policies had been not merely risky, but wrong. Yet Gladstone took too optimistic a view of the good faith and good intentions of other states : having been driven to sanction the occupation of Egypt in 1882, he refused to set up a British protectorate there. Had he not lately denounced Disraeli for setting up a protectorate over another and less important piece of Turkish territory, Cyprus ? Consistency alone would have led him to oppose a similar policy in Egypt ; his belief that the powers of Europe ought to act in harmonious concert led him farther. He set up in 1885 a board of six powers to run the affairs of the canal, so constituted that the British, who remained in sole occupation of the area, were powerless to act unless they could secure the German vote on their side. This complex arrangement gave Bismarck and his successors a weapon which they did not hesitate to use : they made Germany's indispensable support on Egyptian matters conditional on surrender by Great Britain to a series of German demands elsewhere.

This inconvenient, even disagreeable, result had not been expected by the voters who had put Gladstone's liberal government into power in 1880. Nor indeed was it known to them. But Gladstone in office, busied with too many things, lost the hold on the public imagination that his single-minded opposition to Disraeli's imperialism had secured before he came back to power ; and an imperialism less blatant, on the whole, than Disraeli's secured attention instead.

This view of empire had two faces, one kind and one cruel. The less agreeable aspect was once summed up and dismissed by Gladstone as 'mere earth-hunger' : it consisted in an unrestrained appetite for power over as wide an area of the world as possible. Naval power, military power, political power, economic power—power in all its forms was desired, and especially in its economic form. In the intricate and unstable world market which had grown up by the end of the last century, advantage naturally lay with those who commanded the largest resources in raw materials and in markets, as well as in manufacturing skill and in means of transport; about half the world's seaborne trade went in British ships, and British imperialists were determined that their big lead in this respect should be matched by a dominating position on the continent of Africa. Africa in the eighteen-eighties was still very much of a 'dark continent', its coast well enough known, its little-explored interior believed to contain fabulous mineral riches as well as millions of unclothed and untaught people, who might be turned —so it was argued—into a splendid market for manufactured goods if they were properly taken in hand by more highly organized Europeans. Goldie in the west, Mackinnon in the east, and Rhodes in the south of the continent, backed by numerous investors in London, opened up territories so huge that they had to attract the supervision of the state; and in the last sixteen years of the century over two and a quarter million square miles were added to the British African empire. In the same period, the French secured an even larger territory, about three million square miles (an area equal to that of the continental United States); but much of it, as Salisbury unkindly observed, was very light soil—Saharan sand, in fact; while the British territories, the Rhodesias especially, were rich in copper, cocoa, cotton, and men.

Intermingled with this frankly profit-hunting view of the empire was a graver and more responsible attitude, which attracted some equally adventurous yet more sober-minded men. They held that the British were not so much the owners as the trustees of their new territories, and indeed of their old; many of the finest men of this cast of mind worked, by family tradition or on their own initiative, in the Indian civil service. Their self-appointed laureate, Kipling, wrote seriously of 'the white man's burden'; they felt it their duty to take to primitive peoples the advantages, moral as well as material, of a more civilized way of life. Mackinnon deserves mention in this company as well as among the entrepreneur-imperialists, for he was a strong promoter of the missionary activities which accompanied, or even preceded, the traders all over Africa; still more important were such administrators as Lugard and, above all, Sir Evelyn Baring, later Lord Cromer, on whom the weight of practical responsibility for British conduct in Egypt rested. By such men's firm sagacity British imperialism was enabled to bring benefits of immense local value to areas which would merely have been exploited had they been left to business men alone.

With this long-sighted imperialism Salisbury was in strong sympathy ; and thanks to a panic in part of the English electorate in 1886, caused by Gladstone's half-understood proposals for Irish autonomy, Salisbury's conservative party governed the country for most of the following twenty years. He controlled British foreign policy from 1885 till he retired seventeen years later ; though he was not always himself at the Foreign Office, lesser figures there were not inclined to depart from lines he laid down. A great aristocrat by birth, immensely rich, tall, stout, heavily bearded, he seemed formidable to those outside his family circle ; he was also very shy. Few, if any, people but himself knew exactly what his policy at any given moment was (nor, incidentally, has much been found out since, as he did most of his diplomatic business through private correspondence, and his private papers are only just becoming available). Yet his massive presence combined with undoubted force of intellect to inspire confidence in the country at large, in cabinet, and in parliament, in his steady judgement and sound sense.

Able as Salisbury was, and powerful as was the country he guided, he was not so perfect a master of the arts of diplomacy that he could escape entanglement in Bismarck's subtle web of European alliances. He took over the traditional view that France, and after France Russia, were the powers Great Britain had most cause to fear ; and in 1887 he was drawn into a complicated arrangement, of which the half was not known in London, designed to secure the peace of Europe under Bismarck's supervision. Great Britain agreed to co-operate with Austria-Hungary and Italy, by armed force if need be, to protect Turkey against any Russian attack. The agreement was negociated secretly by Salisbury with the Austro-Hungarian and Italian ambassadors in London ; and though Salisbury had got prior cabinet approval for the policy, knowledge of the final text of the notes exchanged was restricted on the British side to the queen and less than two dozen of her subjects. It would be a nice point for a constitutional lawyer to argue what obligation, if any, these notes imposed on later British governments. In fact, none arose; for by the time Salisbury came back to office after the liberal governments of 1892-95 circumstances had altered. Bismarck had fallen in 1890; France and Russia had entered, rather hesitantly, into the alliance Bismarck had dreaded and prevented. Turkish massacres of Armenians turned British public opinion violently against Turkey, where Germany was busy establishing herself in the protector's position formerly held by Great Britain; and when Salisbury caused a detailed study to be made of the strategic dangers that would attend a Russian occupation of Constantinople, they were discovered not to exist at all.

And suddenly, like the single lightning flash that sometimes precedes a still distant storm, the British public got warning of the German hostility that British diplomats had long taken for granted. At the end of 1895 a band of freebooters, led by Jameson with the direct connivance of Rhodes, then Cape prime minister, and the implicit connivance of Joseph Chamberlain who was Salisbury's colonial secretary, invaded the independent republic of the Transvaal, where they were at once forced to surrender. Their raid was illegal and inexcusable; but it was popular in London. A profound sensation was created there when on 3 January 1896 Wilhelm II, emperor of Germany, sent a telegram of friendly congratulation to Krüger, the president of the Transvaal. This telegram seemed gratuitously offensive to the British, who still retained a hazy treaty 'suzerainty' over the Transvaal, and had provided the bulk of the immense capital lately invested in its gold mines at Johannesburg. The dramatic form of a personal intervention by a monarch inclined English people, for the first time, to the view that the German Kaiser might be a personal enemy.

A more important, but much less noticed, event fell in the same year. Since the beginning of the industrial revolution, British steel production had been the largest in the world; surpassed by the United States in the eighties, in 1896 it failed to hold even the second place—it was now overtaken by Germany. So, just at the time when the British began to glory in the 'splendid isolation' in which Salisbury staunchly believed, the foundation of economic superiority on which that isolation was built began to crack.

CHAPTER II

THE DIPLOMATIC REVOLUTION

1898–1907

In 1898 the British, although they were isolated, achieved a striking diplomatic success; yet the cabinet was already inclined to abandon isolation, and not long afterwards public opinion followed the cabinet's lead. In the next few years the international system of Europe was transformed, because the British were brought to take a more active part in its workings.

France could still be treated in the old way, on imperial questions of a familiar type. The British by now cherished the concept of a 'Cape to Cairo route', a belt of British-controlled territory stretching right across Africa from south to north; and the French were toying with an equally splendid project, a belt of French-controlled territory stretching right across Africa from Dakar to Djibouti, from west to east. There was danger of a clash between the two powers at many points; for instance, Goldie's Royal Niger Company came into conflict with French troops and traders pursuing a strong 'forward' policy on the middle Niger. This particular frontier problem was thrashed out by a Franco-British diplomatic committee in Paris from October 1897. The British, on Chamberlain's insistence, put forward extreme claims, which Salisbury's good sense later modified; and eventually in June 1898 a frontier convention to which both powers could agree was signed and published.

They stepped at once from signed concord to the verge of war, over the control of the area that lay where a Cape-to-Cairo route would cross one from Dakar to Djibouti—the upper Nile. The international status of this vast and steaming wilderness was in dispute: the British claimed that, as a former dependency of Egypt which was in a state of revolt, it belonged to the Khedive of Egypt, a creature of the British, or more strictly to his nominal overlord the Sultan of Turkey. To this the French replied that since the state of revolt had continued since 1882 without effective Egyptian protest, and without giving birth to any organized state, the area belonged to the first comer; and they determined that the first comer should be French, in spite of private and public warnings from London that such action would arouse British antagonism. Early in 1896 a French officer, Marchand, set off from the mouth of the Congo with a company of Senegalese; after more than two years' struggle through marsh and jungle he reached Fashoda on the White Nile in July 1898, and hoisted the French flag. There, on 19 September, he was confronted by a much superior force under Kitchener, who had travelled almost as far—from the mouth of the Nile, two thousand miles away—under much more lavish conditions, with an army 25,000 strong. Kitchener had just defeated the leaders of the Soudanese revolt at Omdurman, opposite Khartoum—400 miles downstream—and had come up to Fashoda with 2000 men on the personal order of his friend Salisbury, who knew that that intrinsically worthless village was Marchand's objective.

> Two thousand souls and twenty thousand ducats
> Will not debate the question of this straw:

indeed there was nearly war between England and France for the sake of a mudbank in an illimitable lake of pampas grass, through which there seeped a mile-wide river falling a foot in every seven miles. There was no fighting on the spot; the dispute was conducted between London and Paris. In neither capital was much Nile geography known; in both, attention was given primarily to questions of prestige. The British attitude was stiff: no negociation could be undertaken at all until Marchand had been ordered to withdraw. The French prevaricated for six weeks, while a cheap and leisurely partial mobilization of the British fleet went through; on 2 November the Channel fleet reached the entrance to the Mediterranean, threatening Toulon; and next day the French cabinet decided to give in. Marchand was told to go. The surly British attitude was kept up to the end, which came when another Franco-British convention was signed in March 1899; the French agreed to stay west of the watershed between the Nile and the Congo.

Delcassé, the French foreign minister, at once offered Salisbury a general understanding on the various other colonial points at issue between the two powers; but it was smilingly refused. The ground given was the instability of all French governments. It is true that the French republic had already run through forty administrations since 1870 (there had been nine in London in the same period); but the real reason was the hearty contempt felt, by every one in England who took notice of life abroad, for the vicious corruption of French public life currently displayed in the Dreyfus affair. Moreover, the French had just shown that they were afraid to fight the British, and Russia had offered them no support; so there seemed no cause to fear or to conciliate them. Salisbury, besides, stuck in general to a principle he once laid down in a letter to an ambassador: 'Whatever happens will be for the worse and therefore it is our interest that as little should happen as possible.'

But in the far east a very different situation confronted his cabinet. It was in the far east that most of the quarrels between the great European powers were found between 1895 and 1905; and in the far east a grouping of powers existed which would not have operated in a European context. Germany, Russia, and France acted there in combination, drawn together by a common economic interest: jealousy of British trade predominance. Besides, they had found a potential means of introducing their goods into the China market, a market far more wealthy and more populous than the African, without having their traffic at the mercy of the almost ubiquitous Royal Navy. The goods could go by the trans-Siberian railway, begun in 1892; true, it was still far from complete (the first through train from St. Petersburg to Vladivostok did not run till 1905), but completion would not take many years longer; and then the predominant British position in the China market would come under a challenge the predominant British fleet could not avert.

Two-thirds of the foreign trade of China was carried on, at this time, with Great Britain, and in London it was firmly believed that the China market was of great economic importance. As the total value of British trade with China in both directions hardly exceeded £10m a year, this belief must have rested partly on

tradition, though of course the established position of British
merchants gave them a flying start in the struggle for concessions
in China that was just beginning. In this struggle governments
also took part. The British cabinet, which included a number of
business men, decided in the winter of 1897–98 that one of the
powers active in the far east should be induced to co-operate with
the British instead of opposing them. An approach was first
made to Russia, as the most dangerous, in January 1898; for a
few weeks the reaction seemed favourable, but nothing came
of it.

The British turned at once, in March, to Germany; and for
over three years the main object of British foreign policy was to
secure an Anglo-German understanding. As it was felt there
had to be an understanding with some great power, and as one
was not wanted with France, and could not be got with Russia,
there was really no other choice open; for Austria-Hungary and
Italy, bound to Germany in triple alliance, would not stir without
her; the United States were anxious to avoid all entanglements
with Europe; and no other powers were counted as 'great' (indeed
Italy's inclusion in this category was a matter more of courtesy
than of fact*). The queen was more than half German by birth,
her husband had been German, the Kaiser was her grandson;
she naturally favoured the arrangement. Many supporters for it
could be found in London, such as the Duke of Devonshire (in
charge of defence arrangements in Salisbury's cabinet), who had
a German wife, or Goschen, the first lord of the admiralty, who
had a German father; above all, the restless and forceful
Chamberlain, who took so prominent a part in the negociations
that the Kaiser liked to speak of his grandmother's 'two-headed
government'.

Of course these talks seem strange in retrospect to survivors
of the two great Anglo-German wars; but, from the British
point of view, they had a strategically and diplomatically defen-
sible basis. The marvellous German army and the invincible
British fleet could not fight each other, and might well act in
powerful concert; moreover the mere existence of a strong

* Italy had been 'a geographical expression' till 1860; the Italian state
had never won a war; its politics were reputed corrupt; above all, in an
industrial age, Italy had no coal.

German army helped the British, for it compelled their main rivals the French and the Russians to maintain large armies of their own on guard against Germany, and diverted forces that might otherwise be used to British harm. In 1898 the German plan to build a fleet to rival the Royal Navy was still only a plan, not the instant menace it had become a decade later. Nor was the threat of German trade competition really a severe one—indeed, though superficially the British and the Germans seemed to be rivals competing in the same markets, in fact the area of their rivalry formed a peripheral and not a central part of each of their economies, which were closely interdependent. Germany was Great Britain's largest foreign customer, and Great Britain one of Germany's largest; the richer each country was, the more it bought from the other.

Yet nothing important came of these discussions. They were not handled well by the Germans, who took the first tentative soundings made privately by Chamberlain to one of their diplomats as a sign of fundamental British weakness, and who proceeded throughout on the assumption that, in the end, the British would accept any terms Germany cared to impose because no other course was open to them in their decline. Sure of their own impending predominance, the Germans counted too soon on the weakness of the neighbours they jealously despised, and under-estimated the flexible strength of British diplomacy. After the collapse of an understanding with Russia, which had needed the diplomatic genius of a Bismarck to reconcile it at all with Germany's other obligations, the Germans never made alliances with their equals: they fastened on their inferiors instead. They thought, wrongly, that the British could be made their docile inferiors also: from this mistake came their diplomatic disaster.

Their system for controlling and directing foreign policy was confused. Ultimate responsibility lay with the Kaiser, who might have much else on his mind; as might the chancellor, who stood between him and the professional foreign office. Actual power lay, from Bismarck's fall in 1890 till his own in 1906, with Holstein, an obscure official in the Wilhelmstrasse who had built himself up a position of authority by real abilities and made it almost impregnable by blackmailing many of his colleagues.

Holstein believed that a British understanding with France or
with Russia was impossible, and persuaded his colleagues to
accept the same idea; so, whenever the British made any concession, the Germans raised their terms, behaving like the
Peelites of whom Lady Canning once said that they constantly
put themselves up for auction, but always bought themselves in.
With less important, but tiresome, pedantry, the Germans
insisted on a written convention, but never proposed a draft;
and from time to time suggested that Great Britain should join
the triple alliance, but never communicated the carefully guarded
secret of its terms.

For the time being, the only product of the Anglo-German
talks besides mutual irritation was a secret arrangement, concluded in August 1898, which divided some of the colonies of
Portugal between the two powers, if ever Portugal should prove
incapable of maintaining her hold on them. A good many tempers
were frayed while it was negociated, and each side accused the
other of giving too little and asking too much. It never became
operative. In Germany it was wrongly believed that the British, in
the following spring, made an agreement of their own with Portugal which nullified it. There was, indeed, an Anglo-Portuguese
secret treaty in 1899; signed on 14 October, it simply recited the
ancient treaties linking the two countries, and secured benevolent
Portuguese neutrality in the war declared on Great Britain three
days earlier by the South African republics.

The fundamental cause of the South African war of 1899–
1902 might be described as 'mutual incompatibility' between
the rural, ruggedly conservative, Bible-reading Boers and the
brash, lively, covetous forces of advancing British capitalism,
ardent to exploit the mineral wealth of the Witwatersrand.
There is neither room nor need to go here into the detailed causes :
misappreciation by the Boers of Gladstone's magnanimity in
offering them peace after a small British defeat at Majuba in
1881 ; bad drafting of subsequent treaties ; harsh Boer treatment
of the 'Uitlanders'—the men, as numerous as the Transvaal Boers
themselves, who came to work the gold mines discovered in
1886, and had to submit without votes to heavy discriminatory
taxes ; Jameson's ill-judged raid, and the Boer nervousness that

followed it when the London crowds treated Jameson, coming to stand his trial, as a hero; the clash of personalities between Milner the new British governor-general at Cape Town, a brilliant administrator but no diplomat, and Krüger the crabbed, ambitious president of the Transvaal; and public over-confidence on both sides alike.

The war began with a series of catastrophic defeats for the British, whose generals were as incompetent as their troops were brave. For the public at home these disasters created a sense of insecurity, a feeling of awful gulfs yawning on every side, such as has hardly been felt before or since; it might be compared to the dismay that attended the far eastern defeats early in 1942, had it not come upon the serene confidence in British superiority which was almost universal in the England of 1899. On Great Britain's rivals in Europe the news of the Boer victories made a very different impression. The British seemed to have been caught napping, in an under-prepared attempt to bully two former client states; their whole army, much expanded by volunteers, became engaged six thousand miles from home in country ideal for its opponents, the finest mounted infantry in the world. The almost friendless empire, without a single ally save powerless and half-bankrupt Portugal, seemed ready by all the rules of *Realpolitik* to be carved up by a combination of the other great powers, who bore it so much ill-will for its long-continued leadership and its unforgivable success.

Such a combination did not take place for two reasons, one strategic and one political. The strategic one was simple: none of the comparatively mouse-like continental navies dared to bell the cat of the British fleet. The political reason was more elaborate. Though all the other great powers agreed that the British empire was too large and the British temper too aggressive, each power's interests diverged too sharply from those of its fellows for effective common action to be feasible: each feared that its companions would get too much, and itself too little, if they joined forces with success against their common enemy. Russia and Germany severally proposed that something should be done, but France would not join in. If there was an Anglo-French war, Delcassé told the senate, 'it is not to the victor, whoever he may be, that the principal benefits of the victory will go'. Nor would

Austria-Hungary intervene, nor Italy, frightened as usual for
her long coasts. So the British fought on undisturbed.

It is odd at first sight that the co-operation which could not be
mounted against Great Britain could easily be secured in China,
where a revolutionary movement hostile to all foreigners raised
disorders in the summer of 1900, in which the German minister
in Pekin was killed and the rest of the diplomats there besieged.*
An international force, mainly Russian and Japanese, relieved
them; the German contingent, bidden by the Kaiser to behave
'like Huns'—a phrase of which more was heard later—arrived
only in time to take part in regrettable reprisals. There was little
difficulty in assembling this force because China was without
organized strength to oppose it, and because the powers, though
no less jealous of each other here than elsewhere, had an over-
riding common interest: if China fell into the hands of the
rebels, there would be no China market for anybody.

British participation in the suppression of this rising in China
did something to raise the spirits of the British public, already
relieved by a more successful turn to military events in South
Africa; indeed the explosion of joy when news came in May
1900 of the strategically unimportant relief of Mafeking was of
such intensity that it added a new word to the language. But
this carnival of mafficking was the last outburst of an imperialism
that, as thoughtful people could now see, was getting out of date;
and during the Boer war there came a turn against 'jingoism'
and towards a more responsible and liberal attitude to the
colonies. 'Earth-hunger' lessened; and the services of exceptionally able volunteers who came from Canada, Australia, and
New Zealand seemed to argue for generous treatment of dependent territories. Such feeling was reflected in the terms of the
peace settlement eventually reached with the Boers at Vereeniging.
By an unique arrangement, an indemnity of £3m was paid by
the winning to the losing side, as compensation for farmsteads
destroyed in the fighting. The two Boer republics lost their
independence, for a few years; in 1910 the formation of the
self-governing Union of South Africa practically re-established it.

* The movement's title, *I-ho T'uan*, The Righteous and Harmonious
Band, was mistranslated as 'The Society of Harmonious Fists': hence the
nickname of the 'Boxer Rising'.

Public opinion was brought to another decisive change of mind as the Boer war went on: the isolation in which such pride had been taken seemed far less splendid, and far more dangerous, when the total trained forces at home were reduced to three battalions, and the newspapers of the continent were savagely anti-British. Opinion in fact came to support the cabinet in the view that an ally should be found, though not for the cabinet's reasons, and with no strong preference for any ally in particular.

The government meanwhile dissolved parliament in September 1900, and secured a satisfactory majority at the first 'khaki election', after an unpleasant campaign. The winning cries were the false one that the war was already over—it lingered on till the summer of 1902—and the infamous one (coined by a telegraphist, and belatedly repudiated by Chamberlain, its apparent author) that 'a seat lost to the Government is a seat sold to the Boers'. The opposition was divided in its attitude to the war. Most of the leading liberals, headed by Rosebery, were mild but firm imperialists, and regarded the war as a necessary vindication of benevolent British power; it was also approved by some Fabian socialists who believed it necessary to support a more highly organized form of society in combat with a less. A more numerous, but oratorically rather less powerful, body of liberals thought that the war had been unjustly forced on the Boers by profit-hungry business men, and denounced it as immoral. Campbell-Bannerman, the leader of the party, took this view; and a young Welsh MP, David Lloyd George, first became well known for his ardent support of it. They were joined by the small but active forces of the ILP. However, the country on the whole approved the party in power, which actually secured a majority of a quarter of a million more votes (on a smaller electoral turn-out), though of twenty-one fewer seats, than in 1895.

A reshuffle of ministers in November, in which some old men were dropped, brought a change of foreign secretary. At the queen's insistence Salisbury, already seventy, gave up the dreadful burden of combining that office with the prime ministership, and moved into the Foreign Office his much-criticized secretary for war, Lord Lansdowne. It was in many ways a good appointment, for Lansdowne, the great-grandson of the great Lord Shelburne and of Talleyrand, was the soul of tact and discretion. But he was a shy and diffident man, not a man of initiative; and Salisbury continued to direct the main lines of foreign policy, while Lansdowne talked French and signed the dispatches.

Just before he left the Foreign Office, Salisbury and the German ambassador in London signed an agreement for co-operation in China, abjuring further annexations of treaty ports, as each country had just secured one, and favouring the maintenance of free trade; the agreement was made public, and for a moment it seemed as though the aim pursued for over two years—an ally in the China question—had been secured. But the German object had been to restrain, not to assist, British economic influence in China; this became clear early next year, when Bülow the German chancellor refused to admit that what he styled the 'Yang-tse agreement' extended to North China, where Russian expansion was as active as ever: 'it is all', he wrote privately, 'a (rather clumsy) attempt to embroil us with Russia without getting England into trouble'.

In spite of this check, and in spite of a sharp characterization of British ministers as 'unmitigated noodles' by the Kaiser, in a typical outburst in April 1901 to Lascelles the ambassador in Berlin, they persevered for the rest of that year in an attempt to reach an understanding with Germany—either on the details of various points of conflict overseas, which the Germans rejected out of hand, or in a formal treaty of alliance, on which no progress could be made. The Germans continued to raise their usual difficulties, alternating them with threats that if their demands were not soon granted they would come to terms with Russia instead; and the talks petered out at the turn of the year in an exchange of incivilities between Chamberlain and Bülow.

Routine co-operation with Germany went on, from force of habit as much as deliberate intention, throughout 1902; but by the end of that year alarm at the growth of the German fleet (which the following chapter will discuss) had begun to spread beyond the admiralty, and anti-German sentiment in the country at large was growing. A joint Anglo-German debt-collecting expedition to Venezuela roused antagonism in London as well as in Washington, and the public was glad when gunboats were given up, and arbitration agreed to, early in 1903.

By this time the search for an ally in the far east was over. In the one stroke of originality that marked his career in diplomacy (unless, as is more likely, the idea was Salisbury's), at the end of July 1901 Lansdowne proposed an equal alliance to the nascent power of Japan. Each power would have preferred an agreement with Russia direct; but the Japanese found that Russia, as self-confident as Germany had been in dealing with Great Britain, insisted on terms that strongly favoured herself; so they concluded with the British instead—not without trying to get exceptionally favourable terms on their own account. Lansdowne handled them firmly; he did the bulk of the negociating himself. The treaty signed on 30 January 1902 promised that each power would support the other in arms if it found itself attacked, over some far eastern difficulty, by two other powers. This was soon published. A secret exchange of notes arranged for naval co-operation, on much less stringent terms than Japan had proposed.

Germany's inclusion in the arrangement had at one time been thought of, but was given up; she did not seem to mind, and the Kaiser remarked, when Lascelles told him of the treaty, 'The noodles seem to have had a lucid interval'. The French ambassador in London, Paul Cambon, made a more far-sighted comment: he regretted that, as the Russians were much put out by it, it would make an understanding between Great Britain and France's ally Russia more remote.

Once the Anglo-Japanese alliance was signed, France and England were engaged as seconds on opposite sides in a duel that seemed likely to begin soon, for Russo-Japanese antagonism was growing sharper day by day. Neither France nor England could rely on her ally to consult her, or even to inform her, before taking some drastic step which might bring the alliance into play: so that either France or England might suddenly find herself committed to war with the other—a step no longer desired by the government in Paris or in London. The French could, it is true, exercise some slight braking action on the Russians, because Russia depended mainly on France for borrowed capital; but this brake did not work on all the wheels of the Russian imperial machine. Vladivostok was so far from St.

Petersburg that the weak will of the tsar could not bind adven-
turers on the spot. England had no control over an ally secured
to her only by the temporary interests of each side alike; Japan
had made it clear from the start that in some circumstances,
particularly if Russia seemed to threaten Korea, she would
fight.

With these dangers in mind, the French set out seriously to
conciliate the British. Delcassé was the French foreign minister
for seven years on end, from June 1898 to June 1905; in those
seven years he vastly improved his country's position, strengthening the alliance with Russia, and securing ententes with the
USA, Italy, Spain—and Great Britain. His friend Cambon, the
French ambassador in London from 1898 to 1920, saw him
constantly, and carried on the detailed negociations with
Lansdowne; but while Salisbury was prime minister he remained
in ultimate control of British foreign policy; and Salisbury was
hostile to any alliance with a European power. As he had written
in May 1901, 'The British Government cannot undertake to
declare war, for any purpose, unless it is a purpose of which the
electors of this country would approve. . . . I do not see how, in
common honesty, we could invite other nations to rely upon
our aids in a struggle, which must be formidable and probably
supreme, when we have no means whatever of knowing what
may be the humour of our people in circumstances which cannot
be foreseen.' The governing role that Salisbury attributed to
electoral feeling did not, at that time, exist in any other leading
powers, except in the USA—whose foreign policy then was to
stay west of the Atlantic—and, to a lesser extent, in France: to a
lesser extent, because French opinion was influenced by a
notoriously venal press. We shall notice over and over again this
dominant influence of British opinion on British foreign
policy.

Salisbury's argument, in any case, had been directed against
a firm alliance, entailing military action; Delcassé sought only an
atmosphere of concord and understanding, though no doubt he
hoped for something firmer in the end. In July 1902 Salisbury
finally retired; he was succeeded by his nephew Balfour, who
had an admirable analytic mind, but was too detached and
unenthusiastic to be a wholly successful politician. Now it was

possible for the French to press on: a few days afterwards Cambon was talking to Lansdowne about French interests in Morocco, and early in August they embarked on a wider discussion of differences.

After the customary break for the shooting season, tedious chaffering began again in the autumn, and lasted well into the following year. The number of small points in dispute was so large that the discussions might have dragged on to this day without concluding, had not more weighty matters brought a decision. The credit for bringing about the entente is popularly, in Germany even more than in England, given—quite wrongly— to Edward VII. As Balfour wrote to Lansdowne some years afterwards, 'so far as I remember, during the years [in] which you and I were his Ministers, he never made an important suggestion of any sort on large questions of policy'. Large questions of policy were indeed outside the king's range of thinking; but he was a perfect master of small questions of manners, and his manners helped the talks round an awkward corner when he spent a few days in Paris in May 1903, for he managed to charm Parisian opinion out of the bleakly anti-British mood in which it had lately smouldered. Much more important, diplomatically, was the return visit which the French president paid to London in July; for Delcassé came with him, and it is to Delcassé that the main credit for the entente is really due. During his visit he exchanged in a conversation with Lansdowne the first hints of what was to be the core of the bargain—the concession by France of British supremacy in Egypt, in exchange for a British recognition of French supremacy in Morocco. Cromer, informed of this, at once seized on it as vital, and urged Lansdowne to close at once.

But the talks still dragged on over rough ground. The French clung to rights for their fishermen off Newfoundland—formerly the bulk of their trained seamen in wartime—which dated back to 1713, and tried to secure the British west African colony on the Gambia in exchange for a surrender here. The Gambia was practically worthless to the British, now that French Senegal had cut off its hinterland; but Lansdowne would not hear of giving it up. Cambon counselled delay to Delcassé: 'We've the right to be difficult; the English have a stronger interest to close with us over Egypt than we have to close with them over Morocco.' Cromer telegraphed on 21 January 1904 that it would be 'little short of a calamity' if the talks broke down for lack of decent compensation to France.

A decision was soon brought on by the crisis in the far east. On 8 February Japanese torpedo boats slipped into the Russian-occupied Manchurian harbour of Port Arthur in the dark, and crippled the Russian far eastern fleet. The Russo-Japanese war which thus broke out made keener the danger that France and Great Britain would find themselves taking opposite sides in a war neither now wanted to fight; and after a few tiresome but unimportant hitches, the various points at issue were bundled into three conventions which Cambon and Lansdowne signed on 8 April. France gave up most of her special rights in the Newfoundland fisheries, and received in return, besides some minor concessions on the Gambian and Nigerian frontiers, the Los islands, a group of almost worthless islets—the largest of them eight miles by two—lying just off the capital of French Guinea. Several minor colonial difficulties were settled also. Much more important, the French accepted British domination in Egypt, in exchange for a British recognition of predominant French interest in Morocco; and the two governments agreed 'to afford to one another their diplomatic support' over the consequential details. Some secret articles contemplated the creation of a Spanish zone in Morocco. These articles did a lot of harm; for it became known in 'diplomatic circles' that they existed, and nobody—least of all the Germans—could believe their content was so comparatively slight. They were published in 1911.

The agreement was meant, by its British makers at any rate, to settle local awkwardnesses, and to free British hands in Egypt at a reasonable price—indeed its details, and the lack in it of large or binding general obligations, contrast so markedly with the grandiose proposals for alliance with Germany as to recall Pound's epigram:

> Leucis, who intended a Grand Passion,
> Ends with a willingness-to-oblige.

But as time went on, the two countries got into the habit of giving each other diplomatic support on wider issues than the North African ones for which they had promised it ; gradually, the British became drawn into the orbit of the Franco-Russian alliance. France was able to use the new good-will towards her in London in October 1904, when a crisis blew up, sudden and sharp as a squall, between the British and the Russians. The Russian Baltic fleet, beginning the long voyage that was to end seven months later in the disaster of Tsushima, fired with careless levity on the Hull fishing fleet, anchored on the Dogger Bank. The number of casualties was very small, but the British were naturally furious that there had been any. Adroit mediation by Delcassé between London and St. Petersburg helped to secure a prompt Russian apology, and the eventual payment of compensation.

The war between Russia and Japan provided a series of catastrophes for Russian arms which made a profound impression all over Asia, for they were the first sustained series of defeats of Europeans by Asiatics since the days of Genghis Khan. In Russia itself, attempts at revolution early in 1905, bloodily suppressed, called in question the whole stability of the tsar's regime. No other powers offered to help Russia ; partly from fear of the Anglo-Japanese alliance, no one outside England taking seriously the implication in it that it would not apply to a war either of its parties began ; partly from fear of each other. Yet the manifest weakness of Russia provided Germany with a temptation she did not resist to try to score off Russia's ally France : the Germans decided to smother the infant Anglo-French entente.

The most promising line of attack on it would have been through the Egyptian question, on which the French had sadly and sourly given way. Egypt had been regarded since Napoleon's day as a French sphere of influence, and only lack of nerve had kept the French from joining the original British invasion in 1882 ; plenty of enthusiasm could still have been aroused, by judicious bribing of editors in Paris, for an anti-British agitation on this issue ; but the sagacious Cromer had been too quick. The entente of April 1904 had been accompanied by a draft decree re-settling the almost hopelessly complicated finances of Egypt ; all the powers except Germany accepted it at once, and the Germans did so after a little hesitation. Thereafter, Cromer's hold on the government of Egypt was secure.

So Morocco was chosen instead as the point of attack. The Kaiser—protesting privately, with better judgement for once, against his advisers—spent a couple of hours at Tangier on 31 March 1905, before going on to dine at Gibraltar; and in Tangier he made an offensive speech about Moroccan independence. All the German diplomats in Europe combined, with elegant bad manners, in a haughty refusal to explain or excuse a speech which Edward VII characterized (privately, of course) as 'the most mischievous and uncalled for event which the German Emperor has ever been engaged in since he came to the Throne'. It was made brutally clear to the French that Germany demanded the retirement of Delcassé and a conference on Morocco. Lansdowne spoke sympathetically to Cambon of British readiness to help—diplomatically; Bülow heard a garbled and exaggerated version of the talk, in which Lansdowne was said to have offered the French an offensive and defensive alliance; he heard at the same time of the sinking of the Russian fleet in the Straits of Tsushima. He sent word to Paris that if the French made an alliance with the British, Germany would instantly declare war on France. The French navy was in a state of chaos, deliberately induced by a radical minister of marine; it was doubted whether half the army conscripts would respond to their call-up notices if mobilization was ordered; the French chief-of-staff reported that five years at least must pass before Russia would be in a state to take the field again. So the French gave way. Delcassé resigned on 6 June. He could go with a quiet mind: his work of bringing Great Britain into the European balance had been so well done that it could not soon be undone; and his successor was forced by circumstances to continue his policies.

An international conference was, it was agreed, to discuss Morocco at Algeciras, across the bay from Gibraltar, in January 1906. By the time it met, there had been a change of government in England. Balfour's cabinet had been weakened in the autumn of 1903, when Chamberlain had resigned to campaign in the country for tariff reform, and Devonshire had resigned in protest against it; the remaining team was neither strong nor popular. Balfour determined to try the old dodge of putting his opponents into office, so that they should discredit themselves by the errors inevitable to newcomers before the next election was fought. Campbell-Bannerman displayed unexpected firmness and ability, formed a strong cabinet, dissolved parliament at once, and secured a liberal majority of 84 over all other parties combined at the general election.

He offered the Foreign Office to Cromer, who declined on grounds of health; it was accepted, after characteristic hesitations, by Sir Edward Grey. Grey, like Gladstone, disliked politics—he much preferred fishing, or watching birds; but he was chained to the political oar by a keen sense of family duty, and by the pleadings of Haldane and Asquith, his two closest friends. He was a man of such manifest integrity and charm, such honesty, and such ability, that no group of liberals would willingly take office without him. But he was not really well equipped for his new post. It is true that, many years before, he had been parliamentary under-secretary for foreign affairs—a post of little importance, and less responsibility; but he spoke French badly (though he read and wrote it well), and had no other modern languages; he had never travelled on the continent, and knew no continental statesmen; in a sense, he was too straightforward and naif to tackle on equal terms the sharp and clever diplomats with whom he had to contend. ('The mud of Foreign politics', he wrote a few weeks after taking office, 'is deeper than any I have been in yet.') Moreover, early in 1906, a personal tragedy struck him. His much-beloved wife was killed in a carriage accident; and for some time, as he wrote long afterwards, 'the past seemed more real than the present. Thought was arrested and work was crippled.' He plunged into the routine wrangles on paper—there are always plenty for a new foreign secretary to read up—and the routine interviews with ambassadors, trying as best he could to keep his mind from memories at once irresistible and intolerable. As a result he failed to think things out fully enough at first; and in particular, he failed to notice the momentous consequences of a negociation which was at a critical stage at the time of his wife's accident.

When Grey took over, relations between France and Germany were still tense, and the French feared lest they should suffer a

C

German attack which they knew they were too weak to repel, either alone or with Russia's feeble and distracted support. Cambon was sent to sound out Grey about what help the British might provide if they decided to take the French side in a Franco-German war. Grey took care to point out that he could give no sort of undertaking in advance about what attitude the British public, and hence the British government, might take to such a war—this would be bound to depend on the way it seemed to break out; but, in view of the complicated technical problems by now involved in an armed co-operation between states, he authorized unofficial talks between the British and French naval and military staffs.* He emphasized their informal and academic nature; he got Cambon to agree that they were not to bind either government to take any sort of action; and of course he did this after talking the point over with Campbell-Bannerman. On the other hand, he made a serious mistake in failing to insist that the point was brought before the cabinet, which during the critical second half of January was scattered, electioneering; and, distracted by his wife's death, he did not see the implications of what he had done. Gradually, over the years, co-operation between the French and British staffs became so intimate that an overwhelming obligation of friendship and honour was built up, which in spite of all assurances to the contrary bound the two governments together as surely as any alliance.

The original war in which these talks had been designed to help never broke out: for the Algeciras conference came to an unexpectedly peaceful conclusion, leaving the French in a position that would not deter them from mastering Morocco later. This settlement, a resounding diplomatic rebuff for Germany, as a result of which Holstein was at last dismissed, was secured by the firmness of the British delegate, Sir Arthur Nicolson. Once assured by Grey that the liberals meant to implement to the full the conservative promise of diplomatic support to France in quarrels arising out of the Egypt-Morocco bargain, Nicolson showed himself *plus français que les Français* on occasion, and dexterously secured the satisfaction of all the main French claims.

* Twenty years later, when he wrote his autobiography, he misremembered these talks as having begun under Lansdowne: this was not so.

Nicolson was next sent as ambassador to St. Petersburg, armed with instructions from Grey to obtain the entente with Russia which the peacefully inclined foreign secretary had for some time desired. The really important spheres of Anglo-Russian rivalry, the China market in the far east and the control of the Bosphorus and the Dardanelles in the near east, were left out of court; the Russo-Japanese war had reduced Russian interest in China for the time being, and neither side was in any mood to make concessions on the Straits—the Russians tried, and failed, to get some. Instead, the British took advantage of Russia's weakness to clear some tiresome difficulties out of the way in the middle east; and after a year's intricate work, conducted with patience and adroitness, Nicolson signed three conventions with the Russian foreign minister Iswolski on 31 August 1907. One dealt with Tibet, which both powers agreed to leave alone, and one with Afghanistan, which the Russians admitted to lie within British control. Most important, Persia was divided into three 'spheres of influence'—a Russian, a British, and a neutral one between. This satisfied the Russians, who seem to have feared German penetration into Persia *via* Turkey, and the British, who secured adequately the north-west frontier of India.* No one thought of oil.

The arrangement was attacked with peculiar violence in London, from two opposite sides. The imperialists held that disgracefully large concessions had been made to an age-long enemy, and were not mollified by the announcement that the Indian authorities, military as well as civil, had fully approved the zone boundaries in Persia. The radicals, on the other hand, took much offence that a cabinet which called itself liberal should enter into agreements of any kind with an odious despotism. Grey was unmoved by criticism from either flank,

* For over half a century the British, misled by small-scale maps and ignorance of the ground, had feared that the Russians would carry out the ambition which in equal ignorance they cherished, of invading India through the fastnesses of the Hindu Kush, virtually impassable to a modern army (Kipling's 'The Man Who Was' in *Life's Handicap* gives a breath of the atmosphere). A Russian invasion of India will be feasible whenever the Russians care to build the necessary air transport fleet and bases : not before. The German general staff, a not incompetent body of experts, concluded in 1904 that the project of an invasion by land was 'a complete illusion'; but it continued to haunt British, and Russian, imagination.

and held steadfastly to what had been signed—more steadfastly indeed than the Russians, who did not scruple as they recovered their strength to encroach extensively on the central Persian sphere of influence that was supposed to be neutral.

He was fortified in his view by the support of his staff in the Foreign Office, a body whose influence had been much strengthened by an office reform, prepared earlier, made just after he became foreign secretary. Up to then the staff, following a strict tradition that was over a century old and had enjoyed Salisbury's warm support, had been mere clerks, required to produce papers but not to comment on them. With the growth of business, so subordinate a position had of course become intolerable; and the body of eager and intelligent men Grey found in Downing Street, many of them much cleverer than himself, and not all of such integrity, delighted in their new-found freedom to make comments on what passed across their desks on the way to his. Several of the ablest men in the office had by this time become strongly hostile to Germany, and Grey, who had suffered some German bullying when he had been under-secretary, felt he had to struggle hard not to share their hostility.

From the anti-German point of view, the value of the Anglo-Russian understanding was, or might be made to be, that it established a group of three powers, England, France, and Russia, which could hold in balance the three allied powers of Germany, Austria-Hungary, and Italy: a concept which tempted Grey at times, and dominated some of his assistants' thinking. We must now see on what fear this concept was founded.

CHAPTER III

ANGLO-GERMAN TENSION

1906-1914

'The first article of an Englishman's Political Creed must be, That he believeth in the Sea, &c.' So the first Lord Halifax had written, at the end of the seventeenth century; and the burden of his pamphlet, 'Look to your Moat', had remained a guiding principle for English statesmen ever since. As we have seen, the strength of Great Britain all over the world in the nineteenth century had been created and sustained by naval power; and this power, in its turn, was sustained by an enthusiasm common to men of all British parties to the right of the radicals,* communicable in times of crisis to a self-confident public.

At first glance, then, it might seem that the change in British foreign policy which the last chapter sketched out had been precipitated by the launching at the turn of the century of the project of a High Seas Fleet for the neighbour power of Germany. Such a conclusion would be wrong: though the first German navy law came at the same time as the British shift away from isolationism, it was not the cause of it. There were plenty of reasons, political and economic, to account for the British change, without reference to the German danger—of which public opinion did not become fully aware until, several years later, the threatening attitude adopted by Germany in the Moroccan crisis of 1905-6 became obvious to everybody who cared to look.

However, the British admiralty—always exceptionally well informed on technical matters—had been following German naval policy with close attention from the start, and was aware of the important technical point that the vaunted High Seas Fleet could

* With the eminent, but solitary, exception of Mr. Gladstone, an on the whole conservative liberal who disapproved of large spending on the navy, and finally retired in 1894 on this very issue. Many radicals, even, were ardent 'big navy' men.

not operate on the high seas. This was because Germany's naval architects had achieved the compromise, the need for which is the crux of their profession, between armour, hitting power, speed, and range by sacrificing the last of these : their great ships could hardly operate outside the Baltic and the North Sea. Therefore, they must be meant to fight Great Britain or Russia ; and, after the Russian Baltic fleet had sailed away to its doom, they could only be meant to fight Great Britain. So it seemed, at all events, in Whitehall ; so, no doubt, it seemed also to the German naval authorities. The German political leaders were less definitely hostile ; as one of them once blurted out, the fleet was required 'for the necessary purposes of Imperial greatness'.

The British admiralty could not afford to take so simple a view of an institution that had in it obvious elements of menace ; and was fully prepared with a reply of an original, indeed revolutionary, kind. Under the guidance of an admiral of genius, Sir John Fisher, an entirely new type of battleship was designed, and built and launched with great speed and secrecy in 1906. Given time and visibility, HMS *Dreadnought* could sink every other surface warship afloat, for she was both faster and more heavily gunned than they. (Submarines had only lately been invented, and were small and slow ; their menace developed a few years later.) Her completion abolished all previous tables of battleship strength, and left the British with one and no one else with any. Had Fisher's original building programme, prepared under a conservative government, been maintained, the British would rapidly have established a lead of twelve over the rest, and thus kept a permanent superiority ; but the radicals in Campbell-Bannerman's cabinet, from motives of somewhat ingenuous trust, slowed the programme down. There had always been a precarious element in Fisher's policy—he was a man who enjoyed, and even courted, risk ; and as we shall see, its modification carried danger with it.

Meanwhile we should consider briefly two other sides, both of them significant, of the national defence structure, and look again at the economic and political background of the Anglo-German naval rivalry before observing its course.

Haldane, Grey's closest political friend, and intellectually the equal, in an unusually accomplished cabinet, of Asquith, Bryce, or

Morley, achieved in a long spell at the war office a fundamental reorganization of the army which turned it into an efficient fighting force, if a small one. He grouped seven regular divisions into corps; he replaced the incompetent militia by a territorial army of fourteen divisions, officered by country gentlemen and linked to the regulars; above all, he created a general staff to direct the army's movements in war. He made these measures palatable to a cabinet pacifically inclined by arranging for them to save money. Haig, the best of judges in this connexion, said that without Haldane's reforms the British army could not have won the great war.

It would have been well for the navy if Fisher's brilliant egoism had allowed for the creation of a naval war staff as well. A body so named was set up in 1912, after he had retired; but was not one in reality. The need for it in peacetime was to some extent met by Balfour's most important and most enduring contribution to politics and war—the creation of the committee of imperial defence (1902-3). This consisted of the prime minister, the chancellor of the exchequer, and the foreign, colonial, and Indian secretaries, sitting with the technical heads of the service departments and any other experts they wanted to hear; by a daring constitutional innovation, invitations to its meetings sometimes went also to the leader of the opposition, and to any dominion prime ministers who happened to be in London. This committee contemplated, at length and in detail, the basic questions of strategy, and did its best to find answers to them. An example of the sort of way in which it influenced foreign policy is this: early in 1904 Fisher secured its approval for the re-distribution of the main British fleets, strengthening the squadrons available at home at the expense of the Mediterranean: this made general concord with France, which had a strong fleet at Toulon, strategically necessary as well as diplomatically desirable.

Just as the admiralty had its technical answer to the German fleet in the *Dreadnoughts*, so there was a technical answer available to meet the menace of German trade competition—a menace that was, in any case, largely illusory. This answer was a tariff wall; but it was one that British parties were reluctant to adopt. Protectionism was in process of conquering the conservative party; but the process was drawn out over twenty years, and while it lasted was a source of much sourness and division within the party's ranks. The doctrine held no appeal for liberals, brought up to revere the politics of Gladstone and the economics of John Stuart Mill, and to admire the evident popularity of free trade with liberal and independent electors. In any case, these party quarrels hardly affected foreign policy, at a time when parliamentary control over the foreign secretary was unusually slight. Grey was indeed the first foreign secretary to sit in the house of commons since 1868.

The tariff question was not, of course, a purely domestic matter; but as it was for avowedly selfish reasons that the British, almost alone among nations, followed a policy of free trade, they got no credit from other powers for doing so—though protests would no doubt have been made, later if not at once, had British customs duties put serious barriers at that time in the way of other countries' commerce. The British took pride in pointing out to foreigners that their vast empire's market was open to everybody, though as a matter of fact the bulk of British colonial trade was conducted with the mother country, largely from motives of habit and convenience, but partly because large companies chartered by the crown in London had such big capital resources in areas where development had not gone far that they could establish more or less a monopoly in any lines of goods they cared to handle.

The Germans had no overseas possessions at all, save for one Pacific island, before 1884; the colonies they did secure, arriving somewhat late in the day, were comparatively small and poor.* There is no doubt that millions of them envied a British predominance in the colonial field which seemed to them to rest on accident rather than merit, and a lively anti-British propaganda was kept up in Germany by a numerous colonial league. The activities of this body, and of a similar German naval league, provided plenty of evidence, for British travellers or journalists who wanted to find it, of anti-British sentiment in Germany, voiced in terms to which a haughty and conceited nation did not find it agreeable to listen. The root cause of Anglo-German

---

* It has often been maintained that Germany's loss of all these colonies in 1919 seriously aggravated her population problem; so it is worth pointing out that their total white civilian population in 1914 was well under 20,000.

antagonism lay, in fact, in this clash between German aggrieved resentment against the facts of history, voiced with exceedingly bad manners, and a British attitude of 'What I have, I hold' voiced with a pomposity the more insolent for being, on the whole, politely expressed.

The Germans talked much of being encircled; but their encirclement, which was real enough, was the fruit of their own policies. All the protestations of German publicists cannot wipe out the indelible mark which German diplomats made at the time: the mark of men who meant to dominate Europe, on the way to dominating the world. Such an attitude could not fail to drive together the powers that seemed to lie in Germany's way. By the accident of geography, these lay east and west of Germany —hence the talk of 'encirclement', never a conscious policy among leading men on what came, in the war, to be 'the other side'. Grey even objected, ineffectually, to the use by his sub-ordinates of the phrase 'triple entente', which it became fashion-able among journalists to contrast with the triple alliance. The phrase did, to some extent, represent a fact of European politics; but only to some extent. It is too often forgotten, by people who look back at the ten years before 1914 through the distorting prism of the war, how full they were of attempts at Anglo-German, Austro-Russian, Russo-German, even Franco-German collaboration.

One such effort, in the autumn of 1908, led to a crisis dis-agreeable in its course and important in its results. Iswolski and Aehrenthal, the Russian and Austro-Hungarian foreign ministers, met at a country house and drove a bargain. Austria-Hungary was to annex the two Serb provinces of Bosnia and Hercegovina, which nominally belonged to Turkey, but had been in Austro-Hungarian occupation for forty years; in return, she would agree to a revision of the 'rule of the Straits' which would allow Russian warships (of which there were hardly any) to pass Constantinople. Iswolski went on to Paris and London, to discuss the straits question there; and was much mortified, not only by the brusque British refusal to consider any modification (a refusal based not on admiralty advice, but on cabinet reluctance to make another concession to the unpopular government of Russia), but by the Austro-Hungarian announcement that the two provinces were to be annexed straight away—a part of the bargain he had failed to understand.

The annexation was a formality, with no real importance in terms of power;* but it was a formality peculiarly and deliberately wounding to Serbia. This small but ancient country, proud of its mediaeval glories, had only lately recovered its independence after some centuries' oppression by Turkey. Its inhabitants, racially akin to the Russians, were Orthodox Christians, and blood brothers to the Serbs of Bosnia, who were now to pass in law as well as in fact under the wing of a great Roman Catholic power. Serbia was anxious to resist, though presumably powerless to do so without Russian support; this support Russia was still far too weak to give. Iswolski tried at least to get the problem in front of a conference of the powers, in which Grey supported him; but Aehrenthal used the blackmailer's hold, which Iswolski's readiness to bargain had given him, to refuse. France was unwilling to stand by Russia; and finally Bülow stepped in, in March 1909, and compelled Iswolski to give way by a peremptory threat of German armed intervention.

In this curious dispute the points at issue of real substance told against the points of prestige, on which everyone's eyes were fixed. To annex the two provinces to Austria-Hungary only increased the majority of the subject races against the Germans and Magyars who sought to hold them down. To allow Russian warships passage through the straits would hardly have helped a Russia without a modern navy. Turkey stood to lose only a sovereignty she had not exercised since 1878; yet the Germans, who by now regarded themselves as the Turks' protectors, regarded the insult to Turkey as so shaming to themselves that it could only be wiped out by threatening Russia with a war, which the German general staff knew quite well there would be no need to fight.

The Bosnian crisis took place in the middle of an Anglo-German dispute about battleship strength. Campbell-Bannerman's government had in it several representatives, himself included, of

---

* So complete was the measure of sovereignty already exercised in them by Vienna that the provinces' young men did their military service in the Habsburg and not the Turkish army.

that group of strongly pacific, and sometimes pacifist, radicals who have been a distinguished element of the British left, and the despair of the British right, from Cobden's day down to the present. They were anxious that an international conference which discussed disarmament at The Hague in 1907 should have some positive result; and, to set an example to other powers, reduced the programme of *Dreadnought*-building that Fisher had originally projected. The Hague conference of 1907 was as fruitless as its predecessor of 1899 had been; but only two *Dreadnoughts* were laid down even in the following year. The Germans, who had looked with keen suspicion on every move the British had made in this sphere, seized the opportunity to lay down four; and during the winter of 1908–9 it became known in England that German building capacity was in fact still greater, and that a danger existed that there might soon be more German *Dreadnoughts* than British.

This caused a double outcry in England, both among those who were (or thought they were) expert and among the general public, in favour of a steep increase in the building rate; the government gave way at once; eight new battleships were put in the programme for 1909, and five each in 1910 and 1911. These eighteen vessels turned out to provide the necessary margin of superiority when the need arose. But the building of them raised problems in its turn. They were very expensive; and Lloyd George, who had succeeded Asquith at the exchequer when Asquith succeeded Campbell-Bannerman as prime minister in 1908, had to pay for them by a budget so unpopular with conservatives that the house of lords at first rejected it, and as a direct consequence had its powers to veto legislation whittled down. Abroad, the British answer was no more conclusive: indeed, it heightened the tension with Germany. The Germans saw no reason why the British should have so many more battleships than they had themselves; as their colonial possessions were scattered round east and west Africa, the far east and the far Pacific, they argued that they, too, needed a great navy to protect their world-wide interests. To argue thus was futile, when their great ships had not the range to travel to their colonies; but this point was either ignored, or turned back against the British with the added argument that Germany should equip herself, as

Great Britain had already done, with chains of coaling stations reaching round the world.

Repeated efforts were made by the British, anxious to avoid economic strain, to persuade the Germans to give up a race in which the British had no intention whatever of allowing them to get a lead. None of these efforts had much effect. The Germans made the preliminary point that their naval programme was laid down for years in advance, unlike the British, which was (and is) decided every spring; and shewed no readiness to undo, by any repealing legislation, what legislation had once done. They then protested that they must have an adequate political recompense for any naval concession they made; and much time was consumed in searching for a formula by which, in effect, Great Britain would promise to remain neutral in a war between Germany and France. Such a formula was never found; neither Grey nor his advisers were anxious to surrender their diplomatic initiative, and abandon their decided policy, for the sake of a power they saw many reasons to fear and few to trust. They offered to pledge themselves to non-aggression; but the Germans held out for what was unattainable, a pledge of neutrality. Haldane went to Berlin, to see what private talks with the German leaders could achieve, and brought back nothing of any use. Churchill, still in his radical phase, had become first lord of the admiralty, and said in a speech early in 1912 that for the British the fleet was a necessity of power, while for the Germans, who had the finest army in the world, a great fleet must be 'more in the nature of a luxury'. This remark, obvious enough to a British audience, created bitter indignation in Germany.

These discussions had proceeded, an angry ground bass, while the powers that had once formed 'the concert of Europe' sounded discords increasingly shrill. German attempts to prise the three 'entente powers' apart went on; the Russian court, where more German was spoken than Russian, and the tsar was the Kaiser's close relative, proved a fruitful field to work in. This, of course, annoyed the French and the British; just as a Russian understanding with Italy annoyed the Austrians, and the more public aspects of the Anglo-German talks exasperated the French and the Russians. Each power was pursuing its own self-interest, but felt it unreasonable of its neighbours to do the same.

In this confused situation there was plenty of room for misunderstanding; and a series of misunderstandings in the summer of 1911 nearly brought an Anglo-German war out of an attempt by Germany at a reconciliation with France. The field for this attempt was north Africa, where the two powers had come to a satisfactory understanding in 1909; the method, by an act of characteristic gracelessness, a sudden display of force by Germany, intended to pummel France into a mood to make concessions. A small German warship was sent to Agadir, a port in south-western Morocco so unimportant that no Germans were there at all, 'to protect the German colony'; and the Germans repeated the move of six years earlier, loftily withholding all explanation. The French, under a pro-German prime minister, were quite ready to come to terms; but the British felt affronted, as the principal African landlords, that nothing had been said to them. By a cabinet decision, Lloyd George was put up to make a fierce statement in the City of London, the fiercer for coming from the leading radical, that peace at the price of 'allowing Britain to be treated, where her interests were vitally affected, as if she were of no account in the Cabinet of Nations . . . would be a humiliation intolerable for a great country like ours to endure.' The speech was aimed as much at France as at Germany; but the British and German publics alike, when they read it in their newspapers, took it as anti-German, and the Germans resented it warmly. From Germany's point of view the moment was eminently suitable for war—her comparative superiority in armed strength over other European powers was not as high again till 1938—and that danger was only with difficulty averted by a reluctant French cession, in November, of some territory in central Africa, in return for which Germany consented to a French protectorate in Morocco.

This crisis over Agadir was important because, while it lasted, the large proportion of the populations of Germany and Great Britain which, before the growth of the modern amusement industries, took a keen interest in politics, faced for the first time the probability that they would have to fight each other—and faced it with a good deal of enthusiasm, on the whole; though of course the social democrats in Germany, and the labour party and the radical wing of the liberal party in Great Britain, had other views.

Grey had many difficulties with his party and his colleagues. Too many unthinking liberals took for granted that any conservative policy must be wrong, and that therefore Grey should have abandoned the agreements with France and Japan on coming into office (compare the attacks on Bevin, forty years later, for 'pursuing a tory foreign policy'). The number of MPs with personal or family acquaintance with foreign affairs was much smaller after 1906 than before; and the house of commons was therefore a less suitable place in which they could be discussed with understanding.* Grey exercised a dominating influence there, through the evident sincerity of what he said; but a few radical members observed that there was much he did not say, and criticized him for failing to take the house properly into his confidence. There were more 'pro-Boers' than 'liberal imperialists' in the cabinet, and two of their principal men, Lloyd George and the aged Morley,† were put onto a cabinet committee under Asquith set up early in 1911 to keep an eye on Grey's handling of relations with Germany. (Runciman and Crewe were its other members.)

A more important committee was less official; indeed, it had no formal standing at all. But Asquith, Grey, and Haldane were such old friends that it was natural for them to see much of each other; and no leading decisions were made in foreign policy to which these three had not first agreed. To their meetings was often added, against all constitutional propriety, a liberal newspaper editor, and a most able one—J. A. Spender of the *Westminster Gazette*. This friendly, but irregular, channel provided Grey's only personal contact with the press, whose importance he underestimated; though it had long been the practice for someone

---

* The two general elections of 1910, forced on by the crisis over the house of lords, reduced the liberals to equality with the conservatives; the liberals remained in office, with a majority of over 120 provided by the Irish and labour parties. The new conservative MPs of 1910 knew little more of Europe than the new liberal MPs of 1906.

† Morley was disappointed in his life's ambition, to be foreign secretary; but it was he (or sometimes Haldane) who looked after the Foreign Office during Grey's not infrequent holidays.

from *The Times* to call daily at the Foreign Office to talk to the permanent under-secretary.

Thanks to the policy of giving self-government to Ireland, to which the liberals were committed after the 1910 elections both by inclination and by political necessity, for if the Irish in parliament combined with the conservatives against them, they would go out of power, the next four years were a time of intense party conflict. The struggle was so sharp that the leaders of the two main parties hardly met each other socially—a rare, though not unprecedented, state of London society—and on one or two occasions shouted each other down in the house of commons.

There was, therefore, a tendency for foreign policy to become a party matter, like everything else in the political sphere, in spite of its unsuitability as a field of party conflict. The conservatives, including nearly all the aristocracy and the squirearchy, and most of the big business men and senior serving officers, took up a pro-French attitude, though more from fear and hatred of Germany than from love of France; talked much of the balance of power, and the need for great British armaments to sustain it; and toyed with schemes (which few of them had the hardihood to make public) for universal military service. The liberals' strength lay more among townspeople, nonconformists especially, and their leadership among merchants and business and professional men; they tended to be pro-German, though more from dislike of the conservatives than from love of Germany; they detested armaments, as all good men detest war, disapproved of the balance of power, hoped much of the concert of Europe, and revolted at the very idea of conscription. Many of them still hankered after the isolation that had already been abandoned and to which it was no longer safe to return.

Grey had no such hankerings. But he was profoundly pacific; and in spite of his friendships with the more martial Haldane and Churchill, he was a warm admirer of Gladstone, and hence viewed with deep apprehension the ever-mounting armaments of Europe. He was not prepared to go all the way with his office staff in mistrusting every move that Germany made; indeed, though he knew far more than other liberals about the Germans' bad diplomatic manners, he was determined to be as fair to

Germany as he could, and not to lose any chance that might offer of Anglo-German co-operation.

Such a chance was provided in the autumn of 1912 by an explosion of national feeling in the Balkans.

At that time the whole of Thrace, Macedonia, and Albania, and much of the southern half of the Yugoslavia of today, had belonged for two and a half centuries at least to the once vigorous power of Turkey. After a century of decrepitude, Turkish power was shewing slight signs of revival, after a 'Young Turk' revolution ; and the states surrounding the Turkish Balkan possessions determined to rescue their cousins, the Christian population of these provinces, while there was yet time. The three small kingdoms of Serbia, Bulgaria, and Greece, and the tiny but bellicose one of Montenegro, joined together under surreptitious Russian patronage in a Balkan League that aimed at the expulsion of Turkey from Europe. They were helped into this combination by an Anglo-Irish journalist, Bourchier *The Times*'s Balkan correspondent, who being friends with everybody in public life in the peninsula, from the kings to the customs guards, was ideally placed for negociating secret treaties. Bourchier's exceptional knowledge of Balkan problems was available to Grey, as *The Times* passed much private information from him on to Nicolson, by now the permanent under-secretary ; the Foreign Office staff in the Balkans was a good deal weaker and less well informed.

In September 1911 Italy, determined not to be left behind in aggression in north Africa, invaded the Turkish province of Tripoli, and a year of unsuccessful skirmishing weakened the feeble Turkish government. So in October 1912 the Balkan League attacked Turkey, and to the general astonishment swept the Turkish armies, in a month, back to a trench line just outside Constantinople. Their victories were due rather to the ludicrous inefficiency of Turkish supply services than to the superior gallantry, or armament, of their troops ; but Germany lost much face, as she had for years posed as the protecting power of the losing side, whose armies her officers had trained ; and Russia gained much, as all the winning states except Greece were inhabited by fellow-Slavs. In Great Britain and Ireland, liberal and nationalist sympathies were of course strongly with the 'peoples struggling rightly to be free' ; the conservatives, being in opposition, tended to take the opposite view, and therefore to sympathize with Turkey, which had received conservative support since Disraeli's day.

Grey was able, at this dangerous crisis, to take a wider view than party loyalty dictated. He saw beyond the immediate dangers that arose from actual warfare between excitable peoples; he saw beyond the points of mere prestige that clouded the judgement of so many diplomatists who ought to have known better. He saw the danger that a great European war might blaze out of the embers of this Balkan conflagration, and he strove to prevent it.

The danger arose from the clash between the Russian determination to keep open a south-westward trade route towards the Mediterranean, and a German drive south-eastward, towards the Persian Gulf: neither power could pursue its ambitions satisfactorily without crossing the path, and the will, of the other. The success of Russia's protégés in the autumn war of 1912 seemed to throw a barrier across the advance of German influence towards Baghdad.* This success would not only be resented by Germany in the long run, but by Austria-Hungary in the short. The Habsburg monarchy's problem had by now become the problem of keeping its creaking, complicated, bureaucracy-ridden government machine at work at all; but the annexation of Bosnia in 1908 had shewn that the Habsburg appetite for a yet larger estate might still not quite be sated; and Grey could not forget how near Europe had seemed to come to war over Bosnia in the following spring. Besides, he could see that Russian spirits and Russian strength had revived in the years that had since gone by.

With this danger in mind, he embarked on the cumbrous, but not ineffective, expedient of a conference in London of the

---

* There had been prolonged disputes, since the nineties, over a proposed railway from the Bosphorus to Baghdad, which German business men projected but for all of which they could not afford to pay: disputes as technical in form as they were varied in substance. The German government backed its business men; the Russians took the lead in opposition, till in 1911 (being momentarily out of temper with the French) they closed with Germany and agreed to the scheme. British opposition, which stemmed more from business than from government circles, lasted, rather erratically, till June 1914, when it was dropped. Though the first effective German concession dated back to 1903, little progress was made for many years; and the line was not completed until 1940.

representatives there of all the powers concerned; and he made a particular effort to see that Germany's interests were given full consideration, so that Germany should have neither excuse, nor even temptation, to repeat her dangerous and flamboyant threat of March 1909.

For the first, indeed for almost the only, time in the present century, the concert of Europe managed to play a few bars in tune; that it did so with Grey as its conductor was his best achievement as a diplomat. He was able to persuade the Germans that they were getting fair treatment; and, through Germany, to influence Austria-Hungary against rash action, while exerting similar influence on Russia himself direct. Partial Austro-Hungarian and Russian mobilizations did take place; but a direct clash was averted.

Yet though Grey could smooth over difficulties among the great powers, he had less success in dealing with the small. None of the Balkan states enjoyed their too obviously client status at the London conference, where they were browbeaten by Grey in May 1913 into signing a frontier treaty. They fell out among themselves a few weeks later over the division of the spoils; in a burst of renewed fighting, Bulgars against Serbs and Greeks, the Roumanians intervened also, and the Turks took advantage of the scuffle to recapture Adrianople. In August the Balkan belligerents met by themselves at Bucarest, and signed a fresh treaty. Though at the time everyone said it could only be temporary, all but one of the frontiers it laid down (the south frontier of Bulgaria) still exist today.

The great powers kept up a wrangle among themselves, about Albania; and Grey continued, successfully, to support Germany and Austria against Russia behind the scenes, while putting it to the house of commons that he was simply protecting the rights of a small nationality.

Grey and the new and amiable German ambassador, Lichnowsky, agreed in June 1913 to a revision of the Anglo-German agreement of fifteen years earlier about Portuguese colonies; its final signature was only held up because the Germans were reluctant, and Grey was anxious, to publish it. A year later, an Anglo-German settlement was even reached on the long protracted dispute about the Baghdad railway. Yet no one could regard the European balance as stable ; and as Grey continued to mull over the details of peaceful solutions of minor difficulties with Germany, he overlooked more important, major shifts that were taking place in the relations between the powers. He does not seem, for instance, to have seen the significance of an arrangement made in the autumn of 1912 between the British and French navies. Each government specified that it was not bound to any particular course of action, but the French withdrew their capital ships from their Channel and Atlantic coasts altogether, and concentrated them in the Mediterranean : this practically committed the British navy to protecting the north coast of France against Germany.

Meanwhile, Germany was unmoved to gratitude by Grey's display of goodwill during the Balkan wars. The point that impressed the Germans about the fighting was the speed of the opening moves ; like everybody else, they overlooked the slowness of the later ones, when trenches were encountered. In January 1913 they passed an army law, which would provide them by the summer of 1914 with a far more powerful conscript force ; and they paid for it (at the suggestion of a Colonel Ludendorff, of the general staff) by a special once-for-all levy of extraordinary size, about four times the size of the extra revenue raised by the celebrated British budget of 1909—to be collected, and spent, by the same date. The Russians, in reply, embarked on a large revision of their military organization and equipment, intended to produce an efficient army in 1917. And the French, who were encountering, as a senate debate revealed in May 1914, serious hitches over artillery, decided to increase their term of conscript service from two years to three ; a step which involved them in such administrative complications that their immediately available army in the summer of 1914 was actually going to be rather smaller than usual, while the change-over was taking place.

And the Irish situation, more peaceful in the days of Campbell-Bannerman's government than it had been for seventy years, took turn after turn for the worse, when the elections of 1910 and the parliament act of 1911 brought the old liberal and nationalist project of Irish home rule into currency again. The protestants of northern Ireland made clear their readiness to go to any lengths to secure that they were not ruled from Dublin, and the English

conservatives supported them warmly; Churchill earned their
especial hatred for the ardour of his support for home rule. By
midsummer 1914 there were four armies in Ireland. The regular
British army of occupation, much the best armed, was divided
in its loyalties and uncertain of its leaders. Three private armies
were spoiling for a fight; a small, but not incompetent, body of
Marxist dockers in Dublin under James Connolly; a vociferous
force of Ulster volunteers, over 100,000 strong, under the dominating personality of Carson, one of the greatest advocates and
staunchest conservatives of the day; and a still larger, but much
less well armed, body of Irish volunteers in the south, whose
nominal allegiance was to Redmond the parliamentary leader of
the Irish nationalists, though they were interpenetrated by
adherents of a fiercer and more implacable society, the Irish
Republican Brotherhood. (The IRB was, and is, a secret organization; its public supporters joined in a league called Sinn Féin—
Irish for Our Selves.) Kühlmann, the counsellor of the German
embassy in London, reported to Berlin in July 1914 that civil war
was about to break out in Ireland: his appreciation was accurate,
for Carson did actually write out a code message which would
have unleashed fighting in Ulster. On his way to dispatch it, he
was met by a message from Asquith about the imminence of war
with Germany.

CHAPTER IV

THE GREAT WAR

1914–1918

'THERE can no longer be the slightest doubt', said *The Times* in a leading article on 27 July 1914, 'that the country is now confronted with one of the greatest crises in the history of the British race.' The opinion was right, but the crisis was not the one to which *The Times* referred; it wrote of a few volleys fired on the Dublin quays. Graver troubles had broken out in the Balkans.

Franz Josef, emperor of Austria and king of Hungary, had been dogged by family disasters all through his eighty-four years —among them, his brother had been judicially murdered, and his wife stabbed; his son had committed suicide. His heir was his nephew, the Archduke Franz Ferdinand von Habsburg. Franz Ferdinand had arranged to go to Serajevo, the capital of Bosnia, on 28 June 1914, a day remembered by the Serbs as the anniversary of the overwhelming of the Serb kingdom by Turkey— more than five centuries before, but Serb memories are as long as Irish. The Serb government suspected that a plot was in preparation to attack the archduke if he went to Serajevo on that day, and warned Vienna of it; but, by the culpable negligence of Viennese bureaucrats, the warning was not passed on to the responsible authority; comparatively slight precautions were taken; and Franz Ferdinand was assassinated by a Bosnian student. There is not evidence enough to convict the Habsburg government of complicity in the murder. But the archduke was not personally popular; he was known not to favour the unmitigated domination of Germans and Magyars over Slavs; and many members of the dominant races were glad to see him go.

Those in authority in Vienna determined to fix responsibility for the crime on Serbia, and to seize this opportunity to crush her. Before moving, they thought it well to consult Berlin; and on 5 July the Kaiser gave the Austro-Hungarian ambassador there assurances of unqualified German support, no less explicit for being delivered in conversation after luncheon at Potsdam. Among the several incidents which made a general war inevitable, this blank cheque on Berlin was the most compelling: once they had it in their hands, the men in Vienna would stop at nothing.

Hastening, as was their custom, slowly, they presented to Serbia on 23 July what Grey described, when he saw it, as 'the most formidable document I had ever seen addressed by one State to another'. Forty-eight hours were allowed for a reply. The Serbs, willing enough to fight, but prostrated by their efforts in the Balkan wars, did their best to turn the other cheek, and accepted almost all the severe Austrian demands for inquiry and reparation; on a few points, they explained, they would have to amend their own constitution before they could accept. This moderate attitude did not satisfy Berchtold, Franz Josef's foreign minister, who deliberately forced on a declaration of war on Serbia on 28 July. He relied, as he did so, on the promised support of Germany. In Germany, the naval and military leaders were anxious for war, since Germany's relative armed strength was already past its peak. Several facts combined to make the moment particularly favourable for them: the Kiel canal for instance had just, in June, been widened to pass modern battleships; the special levy had just been spent; the French army was near chaos, and the Russian weak. Also, the international money market had been played for some months into a situation unusually advantageous to Germany. The leading German politicians were not bellicose; Bethmann-Hollweg, chancellor since Bülow's fall in 1909, was a civil servant who knew little of foreign affairs; and the German foreign office counted simply on repeating the bluff that had worked so well in the Bosnian crisis.

This time the bluff was called by Russia. The Russians felt that they had been put down often enough in recent years—by Japan, then by Germany, and most lately by Grey's concert, which had kept their special protégé Serbia from getting all the gains her gallantry had deserved out of the Balkan wars. They could not see Serbia bullied, and not come to her help. The French president, Poincaré, had recently been in St. Petersburg, and had spoken in warlike tones. After characteristic hesitations, the tsar ordered mobilization of the Russian army, which took six weeks, on 31 July.

From this moment the German general staff took charge. Grey had belatedly tried to get the Austro-Serbian dispute brought to some conference of the powers—why not a repetition of the London ambassadors' conference, which twenty months earlier had patched up the first Balkan peace? France and Russia expressed willingness, not without reluctance; Germany said the proposal was unsuited to Austria's dignity; Austria did not answer at all. Bethmann-Hollweg, struggling like a swimmer in a mill-race to avert disaster, telegraphed to Vienna over the night of 30/31 July that the English proposal after all deserved serious consideration; Moltke (the famous Moltke's nephew), the German chief of staff, telegraphed simultaneously to his Viennese opposite number that it should be rejected out of hand, and his advice was followed. For reasons of military convenience, German mobilization (which took a fortnight) was ordered on the first, and Germany declared war on Russia on that day, and on France on the third of August. So the war became general.

The blame for this can be placed either on Austria-Hungary for having forced a quarrel on Serbia, in which not even total victory could bring her permanent benefit; or on Russia, for resenting this and seeking to support the Serbs, for reasons as much of sentiment as of necessity; or, with much more justice, on Germany, for backing Austria-Hungary to all lengths and for forcing the issue with Russia and France; or on some combination of these.

But no blame can be placed, as it is still so often wrongly placed, on Grey for failing to make Great Britain's position clear to Germany. There are two reasons for saying this: one, that he did make the British position abundantly clear, in a series of warnings passed on by Lichnowsky to Berlin; the other, that it did not matter whether he did so or not, since the German general staff and naval staff, with whom the final decision lay, had always calculated on British hostility, and were ready to fight whether the British came into the war or not. This defence of Grey is decisive—against this attack.

A shrewder criticism, against which he has no such sound defence, is that he was not master enough of the diplomacy of his day to keep it from catastrophe. It is true that Grey had not the titanic grasp that would have been needed to make 1914 a year of peace : but who had ? And it is futile to criticize Grey for inadequate attempts to restrain the Russians from precipitate action by a threat that they might have to fight without British support : such a threat would not have carried weight, and Grey was in no position to make it.

Yet though the question whether Great Britain should intervene does not deserve the international importance too often assigned to it, it was of course the subject of supremely critical discussion at home. Conservatives strongly supported taking sides with France ; partly from dislike of Germany, more from fear of the perils which would follow if France were overwhelmed for lack of British help, and a strengthened Germany looked for new colonies to conquer. Hardly anyone outside official circles knew anything in detail about the various British military and naval obligations to the French, which had by now attained a complexity and a completeness which would make it morally dishonourable (though it remained legally possible) for the British to withhold full co-operation. But when the French decision to mobilize was taken on 1 August, without the simultaneous British mobilization on which all the prepared plans hinged, the French embassy in London and the British war office were near panic. Cambon asked whether 'honour' was to be struck out of the English dictionary.

How like the liberals, said many conservatives, to hang back in cowardly fashion from the action that patriotic interests and honour alike dictated ! All their prejudices seemed to be justified by the attitude of the liberal press, which—like the great bulk of the business community—was urging non-intervention, right up to the end of July. As late as the morning of 2 August even the cabinet was still much divided. Grey felt profoundly embarrassed, partly at the separation that seemed to be developing from some of his colleagues, still more at the appearance of dishonourable action towards France. He was saved from his predicament, his party was saved from a split, and a perplexed and divided nation was unified, by the emergence of the Belgian question.

Under Palmerston's settlement of seventy-five years before, all the European great powers (including Prussia, the progenitor of modern Germany) gave a joint and several guarantee that each would respect and preserve the independence of the new state of Belgium. The Foreign Office at least had never forgotten that guarantee—fractious anxiety for Belgium's safety had been a leading feature of British policy all through Napoleon III's reign, to give only one example; and on 31 July 1914 Grey reminded France and Germany of their obligation. The French at once replied that they would respect it; the Germans gave no clear answer. For ten years past, German strategy had hinged on a plan to defeat France very quickly, by crossing Belgium and so getting round the French army's left, and to deal with Russia afterwards at leisure. This plan the Germans did their best to execute, and their advance guards entered Belgian territory on the morning of 4 August.* The British demanded a promise of withdrawal by midnight; it was not given, and so the British also entered the war.

They entered it practically united: besides the profound patriotism that stirred in all classes, even those remote from politics, there was a suitably lofty motive for all parties too—for the conservatives, the highest national interest; for the liberals, the sanctity of treaties; for labour and the Irish, the defence of a small nationality against a big. All four of the self-governing dominions came into the war at once, though active South African participation was delayed by a rebellion of some irreconcilable Boers. Even the Irish difficulty vanished—for a time: Redmond made a generous estimate of where Ireland's real interests lay, and offered his party's co-operation with the Ulstermen against Germany. Only a gallant handful of internationalists and pacifists protested at the war.

Unity did not last long at Westminster—there was a stumbling block as early as September, when the government insisted after all on putting a bill for Irish home rule through its last stages

* This movement into Belgium took place while mobilization was still going on. The importance of mobilization for Germany lay in this fact, that the plan for it included the invasion of other countries. Such was not the case with other powers' mobilization plans (though the British plan did involve movements of troops abroad, to a friendly France); but the Germans did not know this, and feared a Russian attack when Russian mobilization was ordered. Such an attack was indeed mounted, but as an emergency measure, not a pre-arranged one.

accompanied by another bill that suspended its working. But among the great bulk of the population unity remained untroubled for some years : the only object of policy, home or foreign, seemed to be to win the war. So it would not be right to treat of foreign policy without reference to the conduct of operations of war, on the success or failure of which it depended ; or to leave out all account of the system by which these operations were directed.

Warfare is not an occupation that liberals take to easily ; only one member of the cabinet when the war broke out, Churchill, had any personal experience of it. To add military weight, Kitchener joined the government next day, as secretary for war : a professional soldier all his life, with no understanding of politics or of politicians, he was a failure as a colleague. But it was an immense relief to a public given to hero-worship to know that he was there ; under his guidance, it was generally believed, the war would soon be won.

Kitchener knew better. The British army was, by continental standards, tiny—the Germans, for example, mobilized 98 divisions to start with ; so the strategic roles open to the British were few indeed at first. Kitchener, almost alone among the generals of Europe, realized from the start that the war was likely to be long ; Haig, then a corps commander in the British expeditionary force, agreed with him. With few attempts to interfere in the conduct of battles in progress—not, in any case, his task— Kitchener prepared for battles to come, by a vigorous recruiting campaign. The great German sweep across Belgium and northern France brought the leading troops within sight of the Eiffel tower, but just failed to capture Paris, thanks in large part to the gallantry of the BEF on the French left. Early in September the Germans recoiled from the Marne ; and by the end of the year land fighting in the west had become in effect a series of siege operations protracted along 450 miles of trenches, from Switzerland to the western corner of Belgium.

By the end of August the French army had already lost over a quarter of a million of its finest soldiers, in a succession of catastrophic and futile attacks in Lorraine. This made Kitchener's recruiting campaign all the more important : till a British army was created, the initiative on land lay with the 'central powers'—

or rather, with Germany; for the Austrians, with their customary inefficiency, managed to get defeated by Serbia, and relied in future on German support. The German strategists devoted their main attention in 1915 to their eastern front, where they secured huge though indecisive gains in territory; and when winter closed in to save the ill-equipped remnants of the Russian army, a small German force was diverted to dispose of Serbia. The western front was comparatively quiet this year.

Meanwhile there had been much activity, little of it successful, at the Foreign Office. Turkey secretly agreed, just as the war began, to side with Germany; the British ambassador at Constantinople did not discover this till the Turks entered the war at the end of October. This should have provided a chance to re-establish a Balkan league, to work against Turkey and Germany at once, but the chance was not taken: partly because the Balkan kingdoms were too jealous of each other, partly because British action was not properly co-ordinated with Russian, and partly because British diplomats in the peninsula were ill informed; and, by an unlucky quarrel with *The Times*, Grey cut himself off from Bourchier's excellent information just when he needed it most.

No war aims had been formulated by the British, except for the liberation of 'gallant little Belgium'; but as the war went on, it became necessary to promise various gains to other powers—to the battered Russians and French, to keep their spirits up; and to the Italians, who had remained neutral, to persuade them to fight against their former allies. In March 1915 the liberal government decided, with the silent assent of Lansdowne and Bonar Law the conservative leaders, to reverse a long-standing principle of British foreign policy, and to conclude a secret treaty by which Russia was to take Constantinople after the war. An ignoble bargaining match was proceeding meanwhile with Italy, to whom both sides offered strips of their opponents' territories; the Italians closed in the end with the larger offer— Istria, Dalmatia, south Tirol, and perhaps a slice of Turkey— made by the allies, with whom Italy signed another secret treaty in London on 26 April 1915.

Its conclusion had been forced on Grey by the British strategists, who argued that since a stalemate had been reached in France, and the more fluid Russian front was inaccessible from the west, the Germans must be attacked from the south by the Italians : indeed it was put to Grey that if this was not done the war would be lost, and it would be his fault. He did not much like signing away territories whose inhabitants' desires were unknown to him, to a country so frankly out for its own advantage, but he could not face the alternative. As it turned out, British estimates of Italian fighting capacity, in 1915 as twenty years later, were extravagantly high. Another stalemate was soon reached among the mountains of Italy's north-eastern frontier ; and fresh complications were added to allied diplomacy by a series of querulous and greedy Italian foreign ministers.

The signature of the treaty of London was held up until an allied force had been committed to a large action in the Mediterranean : the British and Australian landing on 25 April on the almost inaccessible beaches of Gallipoli. Sublime gallantry just failed to conquer, under the handicaps of severe ground, poor training, inadequate supplies, bad orders, and bad luck. The allies (some French troops landed later) never managed to eat their way far enough onto the peninsula to gain a proper foothold ; an urgent appeal for reinforcements was left unanswered in London for over three weeks, during a cabinet crisis ; and at the end of the year, after more than 200,000 British casualties had been incurred, the expedition was withdrawn.

This was the second decisive battle of the war. The Marne had decided that Germany could not win the quick victory she had planned. The failure to storm the Dardanelles was ruinous in its effects. It ensured that the war would last much longer. It made effective help to Russia impossible, and thus ensured her collapse ; it helped to bring on the revolutions of 1917. Had it succeeded, there would still have been innumerable difficulties, not least with Italy and with the whole problem of Austria-Hungary's future ; but these might have been tackled in a better temper than after three more years of disastrous fighting. The Balkan situation would have been at once transformed ; Bulgaria and Greece would no doubt have been brought in on the visibly victorious side. As it was, Bulgaria joined Germany in October 1915, took her part in the sack of Serbia, and for the rest of the war contained with little effort nearly half a million allied troops, locked away at Salonika (at the cost of bitter quarrels with

Greece) in order to maintain a command in chief for a politically dangerous French general.

One of the many reasons for the failure at the Dardanelles was that the expedition roused little enthusiasm in London. The best British generals were at the front in France, constantly demanding reinforcements which they grudged to a 'side-show' (half the original BEF had become casualties by the end of 1914). Those at the war office also disapproved of 'side-shows'. More important opposition came from the admiralty: Churchill, the first lord, an ardent supporter of the Gallipoli campaign, fell out with his first sea lord, Fisher, whom he had called out of retirement when a ridiculous press campaign forced Battenberg to retire in October 1914. Battenberg was attacked because his ancestry was foreign —an attack that applied with equal weight in a still more exalted quarter. It had been thanks to him that the fleet, which had had a test mobilization instead of the usual summer manoeuvres in July, was not dispersed at the end of that month.* Fisher, violently opposed to a combined operation at the Dardanelles, which purely naval assaults had failed to carry in February and March, flounced out of office early in May. He brought the government down by doing so, as the conservatives expressed total lack of confidence in Churchill, then a renegade from their ranks. Asquith formed a coalition cabinet, keeping most of the important offices in liberal hands; but he had to part with Haldane, the victim of another ludicrous press campaign, which accused the creator of the BEF of being pro-German; and this nearly cost him Grey as well, for Grey and Haldane were old and tried friends. Churchill, relegated to the outskirts of a cabinet of two dozen members (far too big to make the quick decisions indispensable in war), soon resigned and went to fight in France.

The rest of the year passed with comparatively little incident. No fleet actions were fought, for the German battleships stayed in harbour except for a few tip-and-run raids to shell the north-east coast of England. Unobtrusively, but with devastating efficiency, the British navy established a blockade of seaborne traffic into Germany which meant slow but certain economic

---

* It is interesting to speculate whether this test mobilization, ostensibly made to save money, was due to more excellent admiralty information.

strangulation for the central powers, unless they could subdue Russia altogether.

The scale of the war kept getting bigger; more and more men came under discipline in Great Britain, not only in Kitchener's armies but in the shell factories which Lloyd George organized under a new ministry of munitions. Volunteers did not in the end provide enough recruits for an expansion of the army overseas from six to sixty divisions; under conservative pressure, conscription was introduced early in 1916, in the teeth of strong opposition from liberal politicians, but in accordance with general feeling in the country.*

Conscription was not applied to Ireland, where the extreme nationalists raised a rebellion in Dublin at Easter 1916. They had hoped for German help that could not get through the blockade; its loss made failure certain. They determined nevertheless to go on; they were ready to sacrifice themselves, in order to achieve a demonstration of the Irish will to independence that could not be ignored or forgotten. The rising was easily suppressed but the Irish did not forget. Padraic Pearse who led it proclaimed himself the first president of the Irish republic; he, Connolly, and a dozen others were shot afterwards. The severity with which the rebellion was put down turned the bulk of Catholic Irish away from Redmond's party, which by now seemed moderate and conciliatory; the extremist party of Sinn Féin attracted their loyalties instead, with consequences fatal in the end to the English connexion. The executions that followed the Easter Rising had effects outside the United Kingdom as well: they helped to delay American entry into the war for a year. Annoyed as the Americans were by the British blockade, they were still more exasperated by the first German submarine campaigns; there was some prospect, before Easter, that the USA would join in the war on the allied side. But, leaving aside any nobler motives, the American president Wilson dared not antagonize the Irish-American vote a few months before he stood for re-election, and his country remained neutral.

The year was one of prolonged fighting in the west. The only main fleet action of the war, fought off Jutland on 31 May, appeared indecisive; it showed that German gunnery, ammuni-

---

* Simon resigned on this issue, and went to join the flying corps.

tion, and design were rather better than British, but luck also favoured the Germans, who claimed a victory, but admitted defeat by scurrying home and never venturing on such an engagement again : numbers told on the other side. On land, a German assault which dragged on for six months failed to carry the French fortress of Verdun ; and Kitchener's new armies demonstrated on the Somme that they were efficient as well as brave, for they sustained an offensive from July to November against the best troops Germany had. True, they came nowhere near breaking the German line, and lost over 400,000 men in trying to do so ; but in the battle of the Somme Great Britain showed herself, for the first time for over a century, to be a really formidable power on land ; and the German army was given such a shock thereby that it did not face British troops with entire confidence again for a generation.

By this time the social, economic, and political strains of a war of a size and severity that had never been known before were becoming as acute as the tension of the battlefields. The mechanization that had been applied, for the previous century and a half, to transport and manufacture in the countries that regarded themselves as most advanced was now being applied by them to the business of destroying each other. Chemical industries, Germany taking the lead, turned to the production of poison gas ; engineering industries, to the development of aircraft and tanks —tanks, a British invention, were first used at the Somme. The whole adult man- and woman-power of the principal combatant states could be called on to work for the war. In sheer size, as well as in horror, this war was unlike the wars that had gone before ; everybody in the belligerent powers was affected by it, however far from 'the front' ; and the casualty rates were devastatingly high. By the end of the war over six million men, between a quarter and a third of all the males in the country, had been enlisted in Great Britain ; one in every eight of them was killed.

The war was not fought only on the seas and in the trenches : it became a struggle between the belligerent peoples, in which victory would go to the side with the strongest nerves. However delicate the machinery of war, however intricate the economic network that sustained it, the last battles would be decided by the capacity of individuals to endure. As the war spluttered on into its third year, the weakest participants in it started to break up.

Various attempts were made, most of them by neutrals, to get the powers to agree to stop fighting. All of them were futile, since the claims which each side regarded as the minimum to which it was justly entitled, after the trouble it had been put to by its enemies, were larger than those enemies were prepared to concede unless totally defeated : total victory was therefore the only alternative to total collapse. To secure total victory, the German general staff took over, in effect, the task of civil government in Germany ; and with a similar end in view, a deft intrigue by the leading conservatives in London removed Asquith from power in December 1916. With Asquith went Grey, who had spent eleven years on end at the Foreign Office, and was worn out. He longed for the war he detested to end, but he felt so strongly that Germany had behaved iniquitously to Belgium that he disapproved negotiations for peace, since the Germans made it clear they would not willingly let Belgium go.

Asquith was succeeded by Lloyd George, who formed a very small cabinet of five, to meet daily and direct the war—himself ; Bonar Law, busy at the treasury ; Lord Curzon, once conservative viceroy of India ; Arthur Henderson, a leading trade unionist and the secretary of the labour party ; and Milner, who had the most powerful brain in the new government. Balfour, the new foreign secretary, also often attended the meetings. The war crisis was so severe that the new cabinet received warm support from parliament and the country.

The year 1917 began badly for the allies. Roumania, who joined them on a miscalculation of chances in August 1916, had already been overwhelmed. On 1 February the Germans opened a campaign of unrestricted submarine warfare, which was intended to starve Great Britain into surrender in a few weeks—an aim in which it very nearly succeeded. The admiralty could find no useful counter-measures, and contemplated giving in ; in the teeth of technical objections, Lloyd George forced the adoption of the convoy system, and this sufficed (in spite of severe losses) to ensure survival. In March, the tsarist regime in Russia succumbed under the weight of its own inefficiency ; and in order to keep Russia and Italy in the war at all, each had to be offered a tempting bribe—Poland to one, a slice of Anatolia to the other. Neither bribe turned out in the autumn to be adequate.

When Wilson had secured his re-election, and American opinion had been further exasperated by the depredations of German submarines, he led the USA into the war against Germany in April. But a year must elapse before American troops could be available in any quantity in Europe, and it was questionable whether, when they were ready, there would be a European front left for them to fight on. The French army's nerve gave way in the summer. The French launched a much-heralded spring offensive: 'All through the month of March,' wrote Churchill, 'General Nivelle's preparations for surprise continued to rivet the attention of the enemy.' It produced paltry gains, and serious mutinies broke out as a result. Curiously, the Germans never got to hear of them; equally curiously, nor did the British government.

Haig, the British commander-in-chief in France, when Pétain his French opposite number, the suppressor of the mutinies, appealed to him for help, maintained a tremendous series of attacks in Flanders. These were set-pieces in what had become the conventional style, with artillery fire so severe that it destroyed the drainage system of the Flanders plain, and made long advances almost impossible and life itself almost intolerable. Haig hoped to capture the German submarine bases on the Belgian coast. In this he failed; but he succeeded in concentrating the Germans' attention so firmly on the ridges east of Ypres that they did not try a probing attack against the French farther south, which would have brought disaster. For this strategic victory Haig got no credit from his government, which did not understand it and deplored the heavy casualties, or from his army, where Passchendaele became a name of horror.

As the ghastly battle for that ridge died away, two other fronts collapsed. The Italian army on the Istrian border panicked, and ran for seventy miles before an Austro-German attack at Caporetto; and in November the Russian resistance, weakening more and more since July, melted away altogether. Lenin and Trotsky, with a few hundred determined followers, seized power in the Russian capital, and appealed to all the belligerents to stop the war. Their appeal was not made through conventional channels of diplomacy, which as good communists they despised, but directly by wireless to anyone who would listen; it was aimed at the armies and the town workers of the fighting nations, and decked out with the attractive peace slogan which various Russian socialists had used with effect during the summer: 'no annexations and no indemnities'. The formula had its ambiguities —was France or Germany, for example, not to annex Alsace and Lorraine? Yet it also had its appeal: its air of elementary justice was attractive to many millions of people exceedingly weary of the war.

A few earnest socialists in Great Britain had opposed the war from the beginning, as an offence against the internationalism they believed in; their views gained some favour during 1917, by reflexion from their friends' success in Russia. Except on Clyde-side, such rationalist opinions were not widespread. They were reinforced at the end of November from an unexpected quarter, far to the right. Lansdowne published in *The Daily Telegraph* (after *The Times* had refused it) a letter in which he argued that no quick end was in sight to a war of which the appalling destructive-ness could only ruin civilization, to the loss of all countries alike; would it not therefore be best to inquire of the enemy the terms on which peace could be secured? He had put much the same points to his cabinet colleagues in the first coalition a year earlier, just before it fell; the attention they had given to his arguments had helped to bring them down. The second coalition remained bound to the intransigent view that the war must be fought through to a finish; most people undoubtedly supported them with fervour. In this same month of November 1917, the wavering politicians of France were called to order, and inspired to further effort, by the formation of Clemenceau's great ministry dedicated to victory.

Hostility to the new regime in Russia followed of strategic necessity. It was believed in London—quite wrongly as it turned out, but not unreasonably on the little evidence then available— that Lenin, who had got to Russia from Switzerland with German connivance, was a German agent. Certainly the first palpable result of his seizure of power was a Russian surrender to Germany, given formal shape by the treaty of Brest-Litovsk (3 March 1918). Under this, Russia bought peace by giving up a third of her land

and population, half her factories, and nine-tenths of her coal mines; similar terms were dictated to Roumania; and large German armies were thus released for use on other fronts. It is usually forgotten that in the winter of 1917-18 hardly anyone in London knew the difference between a bolshevik and a menshevik, or anything else about Russian internal politics (not even Milner, the only minister who had been to Russia*); and that the sole original motive for allied intervention in Russia was to try to prop up a collapsing front against Germany, and to keep as many German troops as possible away from the western front till American armies could arrive to match them.

As it was, almost a million German soldiers were still in eastern Europe in March 1918; though they were nearly all of the lowest fighting quality. In the west, everyone waited, with confidence as great on the German side as was apprehension among the allies, for the great German attack. Passchendaele's casualty bill had made Lloyd George so much distrust the irreplaceable Haig that he kept back in England, by an exceedingly dangerous gamble, several scores of thousands of reinforcements which he hoped to use on some other front, where they could secure decisive results without incurring such devastating losses. No such front could then be found. The troops he held back were needed badly in France and Flanders; this was shewn on 21 March, when the attack went in and broke through the British line into open country on the Somme. An advance of nearly forty miles in a week was just, but only just, checked—principally by the German transport's inability to follow up infiltrating infantry fast enough over the battlefields. Three German cavalry divisions, which might have been decisive in the west, were idling in the Ukraine. A second attack on 9 April in the Lys valley also almost broke clean through, which would have meant the loss of the Channel ports; but this also was just stayed. Other large German onslaughts, including one that came within forty miles of Paris, were checked by their own difficulties of supply; and the Germans' morale was shaken by the good food and drink found in the trenches of an enemy they had been told was being starved by their submarines.

* Henderson had also been to Russia; but he fell out with the prime minister, and resigned, soon after he got back in July 1917.

Their own failure apart, the most important result of these attacks was that they created, at long last, unity of command on the western front. Milner met Clemenceau near Amiens on 26 March, and they agreed to entrust to the French general Foch the task of co-ordinating the whole allied effort. Foch suffered little interference from any government, and had a steady flow of fresh troops from across the Atlantic—the Americans arrived at the rate of a quarter of a million a month, practically without interference from submarines. In the middle of July the tide turned, on the Marne, and the Germans began to give way.

Their retreat was hurried by an adroit propaganda campaign organized from London. The severity of Germany's terms to Russia was contrasted with the eminent justice of the peace envisaged by Wilson, who, in competition, in a sense, with Lenin for the attention of opinion all over the world, had put forward in January fourteen points to govern a settlement. Effective use was also made of a long article which Lichnowsky had written to quieten his own conscience (and had never meant to have published), about his mission to London in 1912–14: this opened the eyes of many thoughtful Germans, for the first time, to the possibility that the outbreak of the war had not been entirely the fault of their enemies.

Had the Germans been led with resolution, they could yet have maintained a prolonged defence; as it was, their troops withdrew with stubborn dignity before the allied armies' blows. Haig displayed new qualities of generalship as warfare became more open on the British front, where the bulk of the German forces were engaged. The stationary machine-gun was deposed from its dominating role in battle by the mobile machine-gun mounted on the tank, an invention which the British army exploited far better than any other. German man-power was exhausted; allied man-power was receiving strong, incessant reinforcements from America.

Long afterwards, Hitler propagated the big lie that Germany's armed forces had been brought down by Jews and Marxists on the home front. In fact, they were fairly beaten in the field; and the rot started in their own high command. On 11 August the Kaiser, in an interview with Ludendorff—the effective head of the general staff—recognized that surrender was impending; and at the end of September Ludendorff, his nerve completely gone, demanded that it be made at once. Quite suddenly, the Germans ceased to hold up the hands of their allies, who at once gave in; and they collapsed themselves. Most of October was spent in German-American negociations, for the Germans hoped to secure easier terms through Wilson than direct from the powers with which the USA was 'associated' (not 'allied'). At the end of the month the crews of the German High Seas Fleet mutinied, sooner than sail on a last honourable but hopeless sortie against the British; they deserted their ships, and carried revolution with them over north-western Germany. The western front still held, though supplies for its retreating soldiers would have been cut off in a few days had the war lasted longer. The Kaiser fled to neutral Holland, and on 11 November the Germans had to accept such terms of surrender as Foch cared to impose on them.

CHAPTER V

RECONSTRUCTION

1919–1924

THE armistice terms were severe, and secured at once three main
objects of the British and French: Belgium was evacuated;
the Germans left Alsace and Lorraine; and they surrendered
to the British all their submarines and most of their great surface
warships. The blockade went on. The allies moved into Germany
as far as the Rhine; but the rest of the country remained un-
occupied, and the German armies marched home in such good
order that they impressed their own public as not merely un-
defeated, but triumphant—an impression which the Germans
have retained to this day, and which made the harsh peace imposed on them next year seem fraudulent. They thought their
leaders had arranged for peace to be negotiated in accordance
with the whole body of Wilson's numerous new commandments.
'Le bon Dieu', as Clemenceau remarked, 's'est borné à dix';
and the allies did not share Wilson's enthusiasm for a programme
more full of good intention than of precise meaning, any more
than they believed themselves restrained by the circumstances of
Germany's surrender from imposing such terms as they chose.
The allied states behaved as though they were bound to Germany
by no contract, other than the stringent armistice Foch had
dictated; but this was incomprehensible to the German people,
among whom a belief quickly gained a credence which it has
never lost that, somehow, they had been betrayed.

The contractual obligation that lay on the allies, outside the
armistice terms, consisted in a promise they had made jointly to
Wilson in October, during his negociations with the Germans,
that they were ready to conclude a peace on the general lines he
had laid down, with two reservations, on the right to blockade,
which the British insisted on, and on extended claims for damages.
The real obligation on them lay in those principles of natural

justice and common sense that ought to govern international relations. How it was fulfilled we shall see.

Meanwhile, many parts of Germany were in a state of chaos bordering on anarchy. There was a communist rising in Berlin, bloodily suppressed, in January, and another in Bavaria which held out till the beginning of May 1919; and Germany's state was placid compared with much of the rest of central and eastern Europe, where fanatical nationalists and equally fanatical communists strove to seize and to maintain power. Moreover, an epidemic, far more dangerous than its mild successor bearing the same name of influenza, was raging all over the world; it killed some twenty-five million people, about twice as many as were killed in action during the war.

Responsibility for inducing as much order as could be into a world full of tumult and distress lay with the victors, who hastily agreed to assemble in congress. Paris was chosen as the place; as it had been so near the fighting, it was in some ways a bad choice, and the decisive point in its favour seems to have been a minor one—the American security authorities thought it likely to be the safest place in Europe to keep their president, who early announced his intention to be present.

It was thought proper by the British cabinet to hold a general election—there had been none for eight years, owing to the war; and the electorate had just been widened to include, for the first time, all men over twenty-one and most women over thirty. The haste with which the election was held was denounced as immoral by the coalition's opponents. The labour party gave up support of the government as soon as the war was over; most of the conservatives supported it; the liberals were divided. This second 'khaki election' of December 1918 returned a very large conservative majority, disguised as a coalition with some liberal followers of Lloyd George. The next largest party consisted of 73 Sinn Féin revolutionaries, who did not take their seats. The labour party, with 59 members, provided the official opposition. Asquith lost his own seat, and only 26 liberals of his persuasion were returned. The short campaign has often been denounced as one of unbridled chauvinism; but in fact the wilder promises and claims were made by men not in the front rank, and the prime minister's own statements were cast in an elaborately moderate form. As often happens, the qualifications he attached to what he said were little heeded; and he was taken as having promised that the Kaiser should be tried as a criminal, and that Germany should pay for the war.

This was just what most people in England wanted at the time. They had had their lives dislocated, and millions of them had had relatives killed or wounded, in a war whose origins they ascribed wholly to the enemy, having no information before them which could have led them to consider any other opinion on this apparently simple, but in fact exceedingly complicated subject. For the time being, their mood was one of fierce resentment against Germany and all things German; and they were encouraged in it by an angry press. In the armed forces feeling was probably not so strongly hostile to enemies who had earned respect as hard fighters; but only a quarter of the men in uniform cast their votes.

An obvious effect of the great war had been to create sustained public interest in the international relations whose disruption had brought it about. It had been utterly unlike earlier wars, costlier, duller, drearier, and far longer and more terrible than any in Europe within living memory; there had been little romance in it, and no grandeur, only a prolonged degradation. A few profiteers and neurotics apart, nobody ever wanted to see its like again. How was another to be avoided? Plainly, said plain men, by taking diplomacy out of the hands of a few professional diplomatists, at work behind closed doors in aristocratic irresponsibility, and passing it to elected ministers to conduct it as the first of the fourteen points proposed, 'always frankly and in the public view'. During the war there had been much talk, in England, France, and America, of 'war to end war', and much abuse of 'the old diplomacy'; Wilson, it was hoped, would inaugurate the reign of a new diplomacy under which war should be no more. It should be added in defence of the British diplomats, at any rate, of the old school, that they had worked in secrecy not because they loved it, but because they thought that peace could more surely be preserved if the sails of diplomacy were not filled with the tempests of popular passion. The argument remains open; though the British public has got less bellicose as British power has declined.

Lloyd George's principal asset in politics—and he had many—was an uncanny gift for putting himself in sympathy with what ordinary people were thinking, and he went to Paris prepared to work on unconventional lines for a settlement of this new type : unconventionality was another of his assets. He thought that the 'khaki election' had strengthened his hand; to some extent, indeed, it had. But he did not seem to notice that it had cut him off from the only secure base on which a British statesman can rely—the support of one of the great parties—and made him the prisoner of the coalition majority, men more willing to use him than to trust him. During the last two years of the war he had practised his gifts for rapid decision in emergency ; and as a man of spirit and energy he enjoyed doing important things himself. Routine matters of foreign relations remained the care of the foreign secretary and his staff; some weightier ones were still considered by the usual committee of two, the prime minister and the foreign secretary ; but the most important matters of all, the decisions of high policy, Lloyd George preferred to deal with by himself. Little though he knew of the continent, he had already developed a taste for making his own foreign policy, and had an exceptionally able staff of private secretaries to help him carry it out. He went to Paris determined to bring back a peace which his eloquence would be able to commend to parliament and to the country as creditable both to the country and to himself.

There was no one of the stature of a Castlereagh by whom the task could have been performed. Milner had worn himself out in six months at the war office ; Asquith, Haldane, Lansdowne, were old and discredited ; Grey was by now nearly blind. Balfour and Curzon were not popular ; the rest of the conservatives knew nothing of foreign affairs, yet would not stand a foreign secretary who was not of their party. Balfour remained in that post till October 1919, though working for the most part in Paris, leaving Curzon to run the Foreign Office, and deal with problems outside the peace settlement, in London. Balfour was sensible and shrewd ; but he was already seventy. His beautifully balanced mind worked as wisely as ever, but he lacked the force to assert himself against the tempestuous chieftain who was fourteen years his junior, and who had acquired the habit of command during the war.

Castlereagh had taken a staff of fourteen to Vienna; Lloyd George and Balfour took to Paris nearly four hundred assistants, supposedly equipped with expert knowledge. Wilson had a similar team of advisers; the other allied powers relied more on their regular diplomats and soldiers—the military were much in evidence. Nationalities seeking to establish or re-establish themselves on the diplomatic map of Europe sent whoever could be spared from the struggle at home. The defeated powers sent nobody: they were not allowed to.

Of all who flocked to Paris for the peace conference, one of the most important was one of the least conspicuous: a Scottish historian, R. W. Seton-Watson, who really was equipped with detailed knowledge about the problems of the Habsburg monarchy which had just dissolved in revolution. He had worked in it for ten years before the war, and having made himself acquainted with the languages and the leaders of the suppressed nationalities, he warmly sympathized with their claims. During the war he had helped Masaryk set up a Czech regime in London, eventually recognized by the British and Americans as the germ of the Czechoslovak republic proclaimed in Prague in October 1918. Seton-Watson went to Paris as a private individual, and shared a flat there with Steed, the editor of *The Times*; the two of them acted as an unofficial, but effective, clearing-house through which the business of Poles, Czechs, Slovaks, Ruthenes, Roumans, and south Slavs could be transacted. The official 'experts' seldom ventured to contradict Seton-Watson's real expert knowledge, and took much of his advice, particularly on frontier questions.

However, his work was peripheral to the main settlement, of the German question. Negociations on this vital subject were not conducted 'in the public view', but in a secret committee, first of ten, shortly reduced to four—Clemenceau, Lloyd George, Wilson, and the Italian prime minister Orlando. As they had no common language, an interpreter had also to be present; and indeed their meetings were often attended by a crowd of two or three score advisers. Clemenceau, nearly thirty when the great Moltke's invasion had devastated France in 1870, had never forgotten it; he was inflexibly determined to do all he could to weaken Germany for France's sake, and put forward a series of flat demands intended to cripple her. Orlando did his best to impress Italian importunities on his more powerful colleagues. Lloyd George, ready as ever to drive bargains on the spot and act as conciliator in council, was yet oppressed by the need to keep in step with an angry majority in parliament, well described by one of its members (Baldwin) as 'a lot of hard-faced men, who look as if they had done very well out of the war'. And Wilson found that his nebulous views on a world settlement could not be brought into line with the realities of Europe in 1919. His gradual surrenders on what he had at first indicated to be unassailable points of principle had a depressing effect on the conference.

No one was used to the entirely new alignments that had been created by the war. Austria-Hungary had vanished, leaving all the Danube valley in a political vacuum. Germany existed still, but shorn of her military power. The situation in Russia was a dark mystery, pregnant with dangers. Turkey had relinquished all her Arab-speaking territories in the near east. Japan, alone, had large forces on foot in the far east. The USA, Great Britain, France, and Italy had sizeable forces in Europe; but the Americans were keen to return to 'normality' in peaceful trade, the British were busy demobilizing (up to the point the Irish distraction allowed), and the French and the Italians were exhausted by the efforts they had just made. All over Europe, and all round the Mediterranean, small nations newly conscious of their nationhood were clamouring for it to be given territorial expression. Many new problems thus lay before the surviving great powers; and apart from Wilson's pronouncements on which no one else had been consulted and with which no one else entirely agreed, there was no common basis for settlement in sight. It was even uncertain whether, with their enemies removed, the powers which had co-operated in war would feel it in their own interests to go on co-operating in peace; and it was quite unclear what attitude each would adopt at the peace conference to the new, or revived, nationalities.

The conference assembled in January 1919; not till the middle of April was a decision made on a fundamental point of procedure—whether the terms which were being worked out by a plethora of committees were to be discussed with the four defeated powers, or presented to them for immediate signature. Meanwhile, not unexpectedly, the diplomats preparing them put them in the strongest form thought likely to have any chance of acceptance, so as to leave room for manoeuvre during later negociations. In the end it was decided, somewhat hurriedly, that there should be no negociations; and from this error in form many unnecessarily harsh provisions were bundled into the peace treaties. There was a certain rough justice in being hard on Germany. 'A *harsh* peace', said a German diplomat to a Rouman who complained of the terms imposed on his country at the time of Brest-Litovsk, 'you call it a *harsh* peace? Just wait till you see what we are preparing for France and England.'

The weakest feature of the conference—in spite of all Wilson's and Lloyd George's pronouncements in 1918 about the making of a better world on an entirely new plan—was its failure to consider main points of principle. Too much paper—the curse of twentieth-century government—was circulating round too many self-important bodies; with the wartime pressures for instant decision removed, the political leaders were too easily tempted to put difficult great issues aside, and dispose of small but urgent ones instead. Nothing, for example, was done on an international scale towards reorganizing the severely disrupted markets of the world, which after a brief boom subsided into a disagreeable slump, and took some years to recover.

Considering the weaknesses of the conference, and the savagery of public opinion in all the victor countries towards their enemies, the terms which were finally laid down were not as intolerably bad as it was later the fashion to believe. What was missing from them was any underlying sense of moderation.

The European frontier settlement was certainly far more just than what had existed before the war. Danes were returned to Denmark, Roumans incorporated in Roumania; Poland, politically dormant for over a century, was restored; Czechs and Slovaks, Croats and Slovenes, Bosnian Serbs were set under governments of their equals and not of their persecutors; France recovered Alsace and Lorraine, in accordance with the wish of most of their inhabitants. Though a literal translation of the fourteen points into new frontiers was an impossibility, the frontiers arranged at Paris much reduced the number of national minorities in Europe, in accordance with the general policy of 'self-determination' that Wilson advocated.

Needless to say, the Germans keenly resented the frontier settlement, especially on their eastern borders, where east Prussia was separated from the rest of the country by a corridor of Polish territory which reached the Baltic. But this corridor was implicit in Wilson's thirteenth point ('An independent Polish state . . . [with] free and secure access to the sea'), among the terms on which the Germans had agreed to settle, before ever the armistice had been signed. The loss of all Germany's colonies was also keenly felt, though it was a loss in prestige, not in real economic strength. The German colonies were taken over by their con-querors—Japanese, French, British, and British dominions—to be held in trust as 'mandates' under the new international authority, which will shortly be described. The Turkish colonies with Arab populations were divided, on similar trusts, between the British and the French.

In the west, a vigorous French attempt to set up a buffer state in the Rhine valley to separate Germany from France was only with difficulty defeated by Wilson and Lloyd George, who offered instead a joint Anglo-American guarantee of French security, and a fifteen-year allied occupation of a demilitarized Rhineland. In addition, Germany was forbidden to have any submarines, or any new battleships, or any military aircraft or tanks, or more than 100,000 soldiers: these clauses being justified by the use she had made of large armaments before.

A clause in the treaty provided for the trial of the Kaiser before an international court; but he did not choose to leave Holland, and the project lapsed. He lived on there quietly till he died in 1941.

Much the most ardently disputed part of the Treaty of Versailles, the main settlement with Germany signed on 28 June 1919, was the section that imposed reparations.

It is often forgotten how these impositions were justified. They were not the simple indemnity which, by the 'laws of war', the winning side is entitled to exact from the losers, as Germany exacted an indemnity from France in 1871. It was held in 1919 that there had been a 'war imposed upon' the victorious powers 'by the aggression of Germany and her allies', as the treaty put it

in the notorious article 231 which headed the reparations chapter ;
and that therefore Germany and her allies should undertake 'the
responsibility . . . for causing all the loss and damage to which the
Allied and Associated Governments and their nationals have been
subjected as a consequence', and do what they could to repay. It
was at once admitted, in the following article, 'that the resources
of Germany are not adequate . . . to make complete reparation' ;
though Lloyd George had been sharply attacked, by *The Times*
and many lesser newspapers, when he had bruited this idea
during the election, and British opinion, like French and Belgian,
was for the time being all in favour of 'making Germany pay'.

The trouble was that Germany could not pay. It was not
merely that extravagantly vast sums of money were demanded
of her by allied spokesmen, most of whom should have been
well enough informed to know better the limits of her capacity.
The technical economic objections summed up in the phrase
'the transfer problem' were overwhelming. They may be sum-
marized thus. Payment can only be made by one country to
another in gold, or goods, or services. Germany's gold holdings
were by 1919 but a drop in the vast cauldron of allied demands
for payment ; German services, since they would have involved
the bodily presence of Germans, were naturally unwelcome in
countries now ardently German-hating. Goods remained ; and
since the goods that Germany could export were nearly all of
kinds that were also produced in the receiving countries, the
price of receiving them was sectional unemployment and
distress.

The treaty did not make any precise estimate of the size of
Germany's obligation : any sum small enough to have any hope
of being payable would have been far below popular expectation
and demand, so silence on this head seemed the course of
prudence. Instead, it laid down the categories of allowable claims
—much increasing them by adding to the claims for direct
damage, by a piece of sharp practice, the value of war pensions
and separation allowances payable by the allied states. An international reparations commission was set up to draw up the bill
and see that it was paid.

In the end, at a heavy price in disruption and distrust, some
coal and timber and a few hundred million pounds were squeezed

out of Germany. The money was paid in bonds, which gave an ultimate claim on German goods; the bonds were based on borrowing, most of it from New York. Germany eventually managed to evade most of her American debts, as well as the rest of her monetary obligations. These ought not to have been imposed on her in the terms chosen by the treaty of Versailles; but those terms were practically unavoidable in the hectic atmosphere of 1919.

And whatever the injustices of the treaty of Versailles, or of the treaties concluded with the lesser defeated states in the months that followed, the first twenty-six articles of each (the same in every case) set up the League of Nations, an institution which would be able in time—or so its makers hoped—to clear up even the most intractable of international problems. In many countries, allied, enemy, and neutral, the idea had gained ground as the war went on that when it was over some new organization would have to be set up which would embrace all states, supervise their foreign policies, and keep a like catastrophe from ever happening again. Two of the foremost exponents of this idea were President Wilson and Salisbury's son Lord Robert Cecil, who worked in the Foreign Office as minister of blockade under both Grey and Balfour. By the end of the war, British and American officials had produced a joint draft constitution for such a body; and Wilson's wise insistence ensured that this draft was polished into acceptable shape, by a committee under his own chairmanship, and inserted at the head of each treaty of peace.

Nothing like the League of Nations had ever existed before. It had no sovereignty over any of the states which were its members; to the disappointment of the French, it had no armed forces of its own. The vote of any state not a party to a dispute brought before the League could prevent action by it on that dispute. These limitations were introduced in deference both to the general opinion of the day, which was quite unready for any form of 'super-state', and to the jealous susceptibilities of the US congress and of the British dominions. But the League's members did, by signing the twenty-six articles of its covenant, bind themselves to take action in many most important ways. For example, they agreed (by article viii) to 'the reduction of national armaments to the lowest point consistent with national safety and the enforcement by common action of international obligations.' They agreed to submit all disputes among themselves to arbitration, or to the League's council, on which the member great powers, and as many small ones, had seats ; they agreed that if, nevertheless, a member state went to war, all the others would at once break off all relations with it. The most vital obligation (article x) deserves to be quoted in full: 'The Members of the League undertake to respect and preserve as against external aggression the territorial integrity and existing political independence of all Members of the League. In case of any such aggression or in case of any threat or danger of such aggression the Council shall advise upon the means by which this obligation shall be fulfilled.' How the League's members treated these promises we shall see.

The League never recovered from a crippling blow dealt it at the start. Every organized independent state in the world belonged to it at one time or another, with one devastating exception—the USA.

The antique constitution in which that otherwise modern state takes such pride lays down that treaties may only be ratified with the agreement of a two-thirds' majority of the second chamber. Ingenious delaying tactics by American isolationists and by Wilson's party enemies, and ill-advised obduracy on Wilson's own part, secured in March 1920 the senate's approval of the treaty of Versailles—but by a majority of less than two-thirds. So the Americans remained outside the League, to its grave loss: all the arrangements for withdrawal of contact by members from any state that went to war would have far less effect if trade in the abundant markets of the USA might remain open ; and a distinguished precedent was available for any of the original forty-five members which wanted to leave, or for any non-member invited, but unwilling, to join. With the senate's refusal to ratify the treaty of Versailles went a refusal to ratify the American guarantee to France in exchange for which Clemenceau had abandoned his plans for a Rhineland republic ; and the British seized the opportunity to withdraw their own guarantee as well. This British move was an early sign that the Anglo-French alliance formed in the war was breaking up, now that the common enemy had been beaten.

The League suffered under another, equally grave, disadvantage from the start. Many people in important places did not believe in it at all, and managed to keep work of critical importance away from it. The question of reparations was regarded as far too vital to be entrusted to a new and untried body; the reparations commission was responsible not to the League, but to 'the Allied and Associated Governments'. This meant, in effect, to the body known as the supreme war council, set up in 1917 to try to co-ordinate allied strategy, which lasted well on into peacetime in the form of a committee of the allied ambassadors in Paris, sitting, with military advisers, under French chairmanship. Few of the professional diplomats believed in the League. Though one of the best of them, Drummond (later Lord Perth), became its first secretary-general, and achieved the feat of creating the first genuinely international civil service, most of his *chers collègues* in the diplomatic services preferred the old methods in which they had been brought up. Their leaders had the confidence of foreign ministers; and few foreign ministers were in any way enthusiasts in the League's support. So for some years the League seldom had anything to do but work of secondary importance, remote from the central problem of world affairs, the problem of Germany. When, for example, allied troops illegally occupied part of the Ruhr in March 1921, in search of tangible reparations, they did so without informing the League.

However, in the autumn of the same year the League secured an unexpected success. Unable to find any workable solution to the problem of whether Germany or Poland was to own the wealthy province of Upper Silesia, half-German and half-Polish in population, the allied supreme council handed the whole tangle over to the council of the League, which was able to devise a plan for dividing the area. The plan was highly complicated; but it worked well for fifteen years, and this success, which owed much to Balfour's far-sightedness, gave the League some standing by proving that it could, after all, be of use. Yet it is a melancholy comment on Wilson's first point that the success of this scheme depended on its preparation in absolute secrecy.

Although 'world opinion' continued to favour the idea of the League, of which it understood little, most of the professionals in the world of international relations continued to distrust and

F

disdain it. These diplomats' dealings with each other were still much as they had been in 1914, though worse tempered ; and their whole purpose was being called in question by millions of ordinary people, who saw the war as the overthrowing of autocracies by democracies, and believed that in democracies foreign policy should be directed by what ordinary people wanted—and that ordinary people wanted to live in peace. This was true of the Americans, the British, and the French ; but less true of many newer nations.

By this time Great Britain's standing as a great power of the first rank had been somewhat shaken. The peace had created some new powers quite near that rank ; the four British dominions had achieved virtual independence ; the dependent millions of India and the colonies and protectorates, remembering the slogan that the war had been fought 'to save democracy', began to ask when democracy was going to reach them. The British had shewn indeed marvellous tenacity and inventiveness in the fighting, and had assembled formidably large and powerful navies and armies and the hardest-hitting air force in the world. Their industries had proved adaptable to calls on them that had never been foreseen, and their financial strength had been great enough to sustain the whole alliance for some years. But even that strength had been sapped as the war went on ; by its end the British were heavily in debt to the Americans, and the money markets of the world began to centre no longer on the City of London but on New York.

Everybody was tired of effort. The great armies had gone home, grumbling ; many of the great warships' crews had been paid off ; the air crews were disbanded, and their aircraft soon went out of date. Before long the chief of the imperial general staff was complaining that he had nothing like enough troops under his hand for the various commitments the politicans directed him to meet.

One of the most awkward of these was in Ireland. It was much noticed abroad that, as before, British support for small nationalities was set off by a British refusal to consider national claims nearer home. As Mr. Gladstone said in 1893, when moving his second home rule bill, 'There can be no more melancholy and, in the last result, no more degrading spectacle upon earth than the spectacle of oppression, or of wrong in whatever form, inflicted by the deliberate act of a nation upon another nation'; from 1918 to 1921 this spectacle was still usually provided by British relations with Ireland.

Those of the Sinn Féin MPs who were not in British prisons met in Dublin early in 1919 and proclaimed themselves the parliament of the Irish republic. They appealed to Wilson for a hearing at Paris, claiming that the Irish were an oppressed nationality with a right to self-determination; but they claimed to speak for all Ireland, in spite of the notorious determination of the Ulster protestants to have nothing to do with them. So they were not heard: but determined nevertheless to create the reality of an independent state.

In 1920 the British offered Ireland another scheme of home rule, a scheme of devolution, which divided the Irish counties in two, six in the north-east being separated from the twenty-six others; each of these unequal parts of the country was to have its own parliament, with a wide range of powers that yet reserved defence and foreign affairs to London's control. The northerners accepted this settlement, for want of a better, and the subordinate state of Northern Ireland thus came into existence.

Little notice of the act was taken by the Irish republicans. In three-quarters of Ireland British administration atrophied. An undeclared war broke out between the British army of occupation and police on one side, and the small but daring forces of Sinn Féin on the other. The police were reinforced in the middle of 1920 by two bodies of auxiliaries, about 7000 strong in all, recruited from ex-officers; the larger but less deadly of these, nicknamed the 'Black & Tans', soon acquired an unenviable reputation for atrocious conduct. Partly from terror, but far more from national enthusiasm, practically the whole Catholic population of Ireland supported Sinn Féin; no one could be found to give evidence against its gunmen, few of whom wore any uniform. It was thus possible for a very small number of them— they had weapons for fewer than 3000 men—to keep British armed forces that numbered, in the end, nearly 80,000 in a state of constant alarm and uncertainty.

The British cabinet long hesitated between a policy of resolute coercion, which might have succeeded—at a heavy price—and a policy of concession. Though the liberal party in politics was divided and dying, it had in the past half-century instilled liberal feelings into most thoughtful British people; and as the tale of horrors across the Irish Sea grew longer, more and more of them swung over to the view that coercion was wrong and concession right. The prime minister perceived this, with his usual sensitivity; and directed that a truce to the fighting be concluded in July 1921 —just when the Irish were beginning to feel the pinch of coercion sharply. The truce was followed in December by a treaty signed in London. Irish politics have revolved ever since round the question whether this document should have been signed, and its first consequence was a sanguinary civil war between its supporters and its opponents in southern Ireland. For the English, it marked the end of the attempt at total conquest that had begun seven and a half centuries before. Ireland has remained in uneasy but unavoidable partition ever since.

Abroad, the 1921 treaty raised the dwindling prestige of Great Britain; but at home it weakened the prime minister's position, as its terms were unwelcome to most of the conservatives on whom by now he had to rely to remain in power. They began to look out for a good reason to part company with him; and foreign affairs seemed likely to provide it.

Control of British foreign policy remained divided, even after Curzon had formally succeeded Balfour as foreign secretary; Lloyd George seldom resisted the temptation to put through a policy of his own devising. Moreover, he rather enjoyed teasing Curzon, whose grandeur of appearance, pride in ancient lineage, and sonorous vocabulary helped to make people who did not know him well think him pompous and affected by nature. It is hardly surprising that Curzon, a man whose other qualities of mind always surpassed his judgement, did not do better as foreign secretary, when he had to observe not only the manoeuvres of other powers in situations as novel as they were complex, but also the exceedingly rapid and ingenious combinations of a prime minister whose formal education had been as slight as his powers of work were vast, who loved secrecy, and who often forgot—or neglected—even to tell Curzon what, in Curzon's sphere of responsibility, he or his agents were about to do.

Curzon was often tempted to resign, but never quite gave way to the temptation—partly for the selfish reason that if once he left his great office, the many people who disliked him in his own party would see that he never held another; more, because he knew that, on Asiatic questions especially, he was better qualified by knowledge and experience for the post than anyone else in politics—certainly better qualified than any amenable acolyte Lloyd George might put on the south side of Downing Street; most of all, because so many of his friends begged him to stay, and do his best to keep Lloyd George in order. His retention of office sometimes made him look rather more ridiculous than he liked; but it had these justifications.

He was mainly occupied in the search for settlements with Persia and Egypt that would relax British control over them, narrowly failing of success in each case. Neither question attracted much public interest. Meanwhile in Europe international relations were being conducted on a new and more popular pattern, for the time being: not through the machinery of the League, which was kept busy with secondary matters, but in numerous conferences. No less than twenty-three of these which included British participation were held between January 1920 and November 1922. Often they were attended by the British and French prime ministers (Lloyd George did not invite Curzon to one of them, held in Kent); sometimes they were expert gatherings on reparations; always, they were besieged by crowds of journalists. At the largest of them, held at Genoa in the spring of 1922, over thirty states were represented, including the dominions and the pariah power of Russia—the Russians stole the limelight by concluding a treaty with their fellow pariahs, the Germans, down the coast at Rapallo, and the Genoa conference, like most of the rest, broke up without having reached any useful conclusion about a European settlement.

The outstanding feature of the conference period was the separation of British foreign policy from French. France had been left by the Paris settlement in a position of apparent strength, but actual weakness: her industry was disorganized; a great swathe of farming land was devastated; many recaptured coal mines had been flooded by the retreating Germans; the gain in numbers from the return of Alsace and Lorraine just balanced her total of war dead, and the size of the population was stationary, while Germany's continued to grow. The French remained frightened of their eastern neighbour; the British did not, for the surrendered High Seas Fleet, scuttled by its crews, was rusting quietly on the bottom of Scapa Flow. Moreover British statesmen saw that some degree of vigour in the German economy was necessary for any future reparation payments at all; while the French continued to regard any sign of vigour in Germany as a potential threat to France. British public opinion, ill served by a press which had too many proprietors active in party politics, was confused. Many thinking people were already disturbed at the tone and temper of the Versailles settlement, as it was portrayed in the savage and brilliant pages of Keynes's *Economic Consequences of the Peace*; less careful readers, while still stoutly anti-German, did not relish the prospect of a threatened German hegemony in Europe destroyed only to put a French hegemony in its place, and tended therefore to be anti-French as well.

All relations with the continent, and with America, were further confused by the mountain of debts which all the allies had accumulated during the war, to each other and to the USA, the general creditor. The British were both creditors and debtors; they owed the USA less than half what was owed to them by their allies. The Russian revolutionaries flatly refused to pay any of the vast indebtedness, war and pre-war, which their tsarist predecessors had incurred in Paris and London: this solution, though odious to the French peasantry who had originally provided most of the funds, had the rare merit of simplicity. Keynes, in his second book on the peace, proposed that this simple course should be followed generally, and that all inter-allied debts should be written off as sacrifices worth making in a good cause. In August 1922 Balfour, acting as foreign secretary while Curzon was ill, took this scheme up, and added to it in a generous proposal which offered to drop all British claims from all European powers, Germany included, except for what might be needed to repay such claims as the Americans insisted on having paid. Balfour's note was ill received in Washington, where lenders were obdurate, and in

Paris, where any proposal that favoured Germany in any way was at once condemned as unsound.

The French under Poincaré indeed determined, if they could not secure adequate payments from Germany—and the Germans frequently defaulted in the payments they should have made, in kind and in cash—that Germany should be ruined. With the alternative aims of securing 'productive pledges' or of destroying the core of the German economy, in January 1923 they invaded the industrial belt of the Ruhr. German non-co-operation kept them from their first objective, but a complete collapse of the German currency seemed, for the time being, to achieve their second.

This invasion, of very doubtful legality, was disapproved by the British government and people alike; but they were in no position to do anything to stop it. Besides, a new government had lately come to power in London, as the result of a crisis at the other end of Europe to which we must now turn.

The vast bulk of the Ottoman empire had been much carved up, in prospect, between the allies during the war; Turkey's main role in the fighting had been to engage British and Russian troops who would have been better employed, once the Dardanelles had not been carried, on more important fronts. The Turkish collapse of October 1918 seemed complete; the sprawling body of the Turkish state waited passively for the surgery of peace-making.

Great Britain kept on the protectorate declared over Egypt in December 1914, after Turkey's entry into the war; Arabia was made independent; Syria and Mesopotamia (Iraq) became French and British mandates respectively. In Palestine the British prepared much future difficulty for themselves by a declaration which Amery wrote, and Balfour made, in 1917, that they would arrange for a Jewish national home there without harming the existing Arab settlers: two aims which turned out incompatible. More interest was shewn in 1919 in those Armenians who had survived the massacre of 1915 in which the Turks had killed nearly a million people, knowing that all the powers of Europe were busy at the war. It was at first hoped that the USA would undertake a mandate over Armenia. The mandate scheme indeed had originally been proposed to assist such comparatively skilled and cultured people as the Armenians, the Arabs, and the smaller races of south-eastern Europe towards self-government, rather than to provide for the administration of African swamps and remote Pacific islands. Such a hope did not of course survive the sharp American turn towards isolation, and the only great power inclined to do anything for the Armenians was Russia, not a member of the League, and anathema for the time being to all the others.

In an apparently prostrate Turkey there nevertheless arose a nationalist movement of exceptional vigour, which secured exceptional success. Its leader Kamal was not himself a Turk: part Albanian and part Macedonian by birth, his origins were humble; but that has never barred advancement for anyone in Turkey. As a professional soldier, he had distinguished himself at Gallipoli; his steady nerve, as the first divisional commander on the spot, had helped to repulse the initial British land assault.

By the end of 1919 the authority of the sultan's government in Constantinople hardly extended beyond the range of the eye from the city's minarets. A few British troops held Constantinople and the Dardanelles; the French and the Italians had some forces in southern Turkey; western European opinion was in general indifferent to what went on there. The only large army in the country was a Greek one, based on Smyrna, which had arrived in reply to an invitation from Lloyd George to his friend Venizelos, the Greek prime minister, and had in a few months acquired a bad reputation for atrocities, though it had beaten back Turkish nationalist forces against whom it made equally grave charges. The whole interior of Anatolia was under the domination of Kamal.

In 1920 he organized his revolution. A peace treaty prepared for Turkey in Paris was signed by the Constantinople government in August, but repudiated by the Kamalists—though they repudiated at the same time any claim to Arab-populated areas. At the end of the year Venizelos unexpectedly fell from power, and a less pro-British and less efficient government succeeded him in Athens. The Greeks advanced into the interior in the following summer, but were repulsed by Kamal in September 1921, and began to retreat. The French, behind the backs of everyone else, came to terms with the Kamalists; and the Greek retreat, after a long pause, became a rout. By 16 September 1922 the only Greeks left in Smyrna were prisoners or corpses, and the Turkish nationalists appeared that day close to the British lines at Çanak, near Troy, which were held by only a few hundred men.

At this desperate moment Curzon retired, as was increasingly becoming the custom in England, to spend from Saturday to Monday in the country. Lloyd George stayed in London, with a group of resolute colleagues that included Churchill; and Churchill was deputed by them to draft a pungent communiqué to the press, threatening Kamal with the armed might of the whole empire if he attacked. The threat was not as idle as it seemed to Churchill's opponents—for weeks thereafter the Australian, Canadian, and New Zealand governments were getting volunteers by the thousand—and it duly impressed Kamal, whose men pressed close up to the British wire but did not fire a shot. At the end of the month the cabinet charged Harington, the general in command at the straits, with an ultimatum to Kamal; with excellent judgement, he never presented it, but secured instead an armistice, and the danger passed away.

Yet that danger of war should have arisen, in a distant quarrel which seemed to be of the old, and now unpopular, imperialist type, exasperated British opinion of all parties; under the weight of that exasperation, Lloyd George fell from power. (He lived till 1945, but never held office again.) Bonar Law emerged from retirement to form a purely conservative cabinet, from which some of the ablest members of his party held back, feeling they were too closely associated with the late government; and he secured a majority of nearly ninety at a general election in November.

Curzon remained at the Foreign Office. As his new prime minister's only interest in foreign affairs was in the debt settlement, Curzon was able at last to conduct a policy of his own. By sheer skill in chairmanship and force of personality he dominated an eight-power conference at Lausanne, which settled the Turkish problem and secured by negociation the most durable and satisfactory of the peace treaties. This success did much to restore the prestige of Great Britain, in Asia even more than in Europe, at a time when Asiatic opinion was beginning to be much more important than before. For Curzon's own prestige it did not do quite enough. The height of ambition for most politicians is to sit in a cabinet; he was one of the few whose abilities entitle them to hope that they may lead one. The supreme disappointment of his life came in May 1923, when Bonar Law, a very sick man, resigned. Curzon received a summons to London from the king's secretary —to be told that the new prime minister was to be Stanley Baldwin, whom he described as 'a man of no experience. And of the utmost insignificance'. The ostensible cause for leaving Curzon out of first place was the reasonable objection of the labour party that it had hardly any members in Curzon's house of parliament; it may be doubted too whether he could have carried country or party with him as a prime minister needs to do.

He continued to support Baldwin cheerfully, after the first shock, and conducted a calm and conciliatory foreign policy; but the government only lasted a few months. In the autumn Baldwin unexpectedly dissolved parliament again; he was a protectionist himself, and wanted to introduce a tariff, for which he felt he needed authority from the electorate. This authority he did not get; though the conservatives won more seats than either liberals or labour, they had no majority over both. Ramsay MacDonald was called on to form the first labour government.

Very few of its members had ever sat in cabinet before. Haldane changed over from the liberals, became lord chancellor, and presided over the committee of imperial defence. Mac-Donald took the foreign secretaryship as well as the post of prime minister, a burden for which he was not well qualified, as he was a bad organizer of his time. His type of man had never been seen in either office before: he had started absolutely at the bottom of the social scale, the illegitimate son of a Scottish crofter, and had come forward by a combination of brain-power, hard work, and genuine concern for 'the under-privileged', combined with a fine presence and natural good manners. Though he knew something of the continent, he suffered under a fatal handicap as foreign minister: he loved imprecision, and hated tying himself down to a policy. As leader of a government, he had to face the additional disadvantages of inexperienced colleagues, weak support in parliament, and a hostile press.

The most important feature in his foreign policy was his

treatment of Russia; and to explain this it is necessary to go back some years.

It has not been altogether inappropriate to leave the Russian question on one side while discussing the peace settlement, for that was what everybody did at the time. None of the politicians of western Europe, or America, could make head or tail of what was going on there; sources of news were few, and seldom reliable; little of what news there was seemed pleasant. The communists who had seized power in 1917 seemed to go out of their way to denounce all other governments as moribund and corrupt; and indeed have always underestimated both the strength of the capitalist system they oppose and the tolerance of it by the European factory workers on whose support they relied for an imminent revolution.

It will be recalled that in the winter of 1917–18 small allied and American forces had gone to the outskirts of Russia, to try and keep some sort of front open against the central powers. The end of the main war removed the original object of these expeditions; but they were kept on, for other reasons, for some months. Though none had been sent there with the object of supporting capitalism against communism, the Russian communists—not unexpectedly on their premises—believed the contrary; and no Russian government has ever shown full confidence in any 'interventionist' country since. A few far-sighted allied politicians may possibly already have foreseen difficulties with a communist government controlling all Russia, if it was not at once put down; far more people were inclined to hostility to a regime under which the tsar and his family had been murdered (probably, it now appears, on directions from Moscow, the capital of the new state). But the general expectation was that Lenin's regime must shortly crumble away; indeed, civil war was already being actively waged against it by Russians of many kinds, ranging from noblemen anxious to maintain the privileges of their class to liberals and moderate socialists exasperated by Lenin's refusal to let an elected assembly decide how the country should be run. It was from this civil war that the real difficulty about withdrawing from Russia arose. As is usual in such fighting, no mercy was shewn by either side to any of its captured opponents. The British troops in north

Russia provided the only militarily reliable element there on the anti-revolutionary side; if they were withdrawn, what would happen to the Russians of all ages and both sexes who were sheltering behind them?

Nevertheless, the British forces at Archangel and Murmansk were withdrawn in the summer of 1919, under cover of a brisk offensive conducted by two brigades of volunteers, who were withdrawn thereafter without trouble, when as many Russians as wanted to do so had taken ship for England. Churchill, the one resolute interventionist among British ministers, had raised the brigades for just this purpose, in the teeth of sharp criticism in parliament and the press; and claimed with truth that his action forestalled a massacre.

In southern Russia the French occupied Odessa, and the 'white army' of General Denikin advanced far inland. It was fairly lavishly equipped with British and French munitions for which the original owners had no other use; and a number of British technical advisers accompanied it. But the French forces at its main base became, in the phrase of the day, 'infected with bolshevism', and had to be withdrawn; and in the autumn of 1919 Denikin's forces melted away under the attacks of the 'red army' which Trotsky had conjured up out of nothing at all. By the end of 1919 there were no British troops left in Russia.

In the summer of the following year, the Poles, seeking wider territories, invaded western Russia. The red army, anxious for closer contact with Germany, which was still regarded as the most hopeful spot for the next revolution, counter-attacked vigorously. Curzon offered mediation in June, which the Russians refused; in July he offered support to the Poles if the Russians advanced deep into Poland. They did so at the end of the month, and by early August they were within a few miles of Warsaw. No British support appeared; instead, a French general gave the Poles useful advice, and they drove the Russians back without further aid.

Curzon should not have promised what he was not going to perform. 'A menace which is not intended to be executed, is an engine which Great Britain should never condescend to employ', as Canning had laid down long ago; but it was hardly Curzon's fault that he could not perform it. While the politicians and the potentates of Europe were baffled and confused by the course of the Russian revolution, simpler people thought they knew what bolshevism meant. Millions of working men all over Europe—and beyond—saw it as just a revolt of the under-dogs against the 'boss class', and as under-dogs they rejoiced at it. Of course, being honest and warm-hearted folk, they did not approve of murder or terrorism—in normal times; but times had not been normal in the Russia of 1917, and anyhow the Russians (wild people, and far away) should be left to run their own affairs as they chose.

Strong, though not very articulate, sympathy for the Russian revolutionaries was widespread in England, Wales, and Scotland by the summer of 1920; and, chiefly under trade union inspiration, it took active political form behind the slogan 'Hands off Russia'. (The communist party of Great Britain was not formed till 31 July that year.) In line with this slogan, dockers refused to load cargoes of munitions for Poland; Ernest Bevin first achieved prominence as one of the leaders in this widespread and spontaneous movement. It was entirely effective: no more British help could go to the Poles. And from this movement can be dated the firm conviction on the British left, still vigorous to this day in spite of variations in strength, that the Russian government, dedicated as it is to the building of socialism, is worthy of a respect and indeed an affection that cannot be given to the governments of aggressively capitalist great powers. This genuine difference on a point of foreign policy has been more noticeable, and more important, than the milder differences in sentiment that had separated, before the war, pro-Turkish conservatives from anti-Russian liberals.

Some Russian state trading agents were already in England in May of 1920, and may indeed have helped to foment the 'Hands off Russia' campaign. In March 1921 Lloyd George concluded a trade agreement with them (forgetting to tell Curzon, till the last moment, that he was doing so); but the volume of trade that resulted was not large, and Anglo-Russian relations remained informal and unofficial, for the conservatives were unwilling to accord recognition as of right to what most of them had come to regard as a murderous regime. This uneasy situation was ended as soon as the labour government came to power: after an interval of more than six years, full diplomatic relations were restored by treaty between Great Britain and Russia in 1924.

MacDonald and his party got small benefit from this. In October, finding life impossible with no majority in the commons, they had to fight a general election, the third in three years; and shortly before polling day the electors were astonished by the publication of what appeared to be an instruction from Zinoviev, a leading figure in Moscow, to the British communists, urging them to press for ratification of the Russian treaty as an instrument of class war. As it appeared in the press with a copy of a letter from the Foreign Office to the Russian *chargé d'affaires*, protesting at it, it seemed to the public to be genuine; later it looked like the forgery the Russians said it was (though a cabinet committee next year decided that it was authentic). Its origins remain obscure; but if it was a forgery it served its purpose, for in the new parliament the conservatives had a majority of two hundred. It is important to note that the labour vote rose by a million (though labour lost forty-two seats); the real losers in the election were the liberals, who returned hardly two score MPs.

CHAPTER VI

COVENANTS WITHOUT THE SWORD

1924–1932

BECAUSE the first labour government had had no majority in parliament, it had been unable to carry out the reforms it desired at home ; it was not the less keen to make such impress as it could in foreign affairs. Russia was not the only field of labour interest here. Up to 1914 the party had belonged to the socialist international, which had ineffectively sought to avert the war by a general strike, and with the decline of the liberals it came to absorb more and more of the radical internationalists of Cobdenite views. Scores of thousands of socialists believed that capitalism was in itself a cause of war because it promoted competition for markets and excessive spending on armaments, that patriotism by itself was an old-fashioned virtue, and that permanent peace would soon be brought in sight in a world of socialist governments which would co-operate amicably with each other.

The French elections of May 1924 brought Herriot, a socialist of similar views, to power in France. He and MacDonald joined in putting into effect the first intelligent scheme for reparations, which had been drawn up by an expert committee under an American general, Dawes. The French receded from their extreme demands, and the Germans from their extreme reluctance to pay ; American banks lent the money ; and the sums that passed were moderate, increasing from £50m in the first to £125m in the fifth year of the settlement. These contrasted with the fabulous figures current at the end of the war, when a total German liability of £24,000m was called reasonable.

MacDonald's next object was to try to do something to restore confidence in the League of Nations, which had suffered a setback in the autumn of 1923. Italian troops had bombarded Corfu, in revenge for the murder of an Italian general on Greece's wild north-western frontier ; the Greeks had appealed to the League ; the League, shirking its responsibilities, had left the complaint to the conference of ambassadors. They, following a decision of Curzon's which it is impossible to defend, ordered Greece to pay £500,000 compensation to Italy. This was the first success in foreign policy of Mussolini, the adventurer who had lately seized autocratic power in Rome.

MacDonald believed in the League; his party's chief organizer, Arthur Henderson, home secretary in 1924, believed in it too, and determined to make it work. The point they had to meet, if they could, was this: the League's many enemies had begun to talk of a 'gap in the covenant', a flaw in the League's constitution which still left it open to its members to wage war on each other. It is true that such a flaw did exist—if one assumed the possibility that an aggressive state could sustain its people's will to war for nine months on end in time of peace. In fact such circumstances never did arise, and no aggressor ever tried to take advantage of the 'gap'. Yet there it was said to be; and to make sure that it was closed, a League committee under Masaryk's right-hand man, the nimble and ingenious Beneš, drafted the Geneva protocol. This laid down at some length—it ran to twenty-one articles—that no alternative of war was ever to be left open to the powers that signed it: all disputes were to go to arbitration, and any state which refused to accept this at any stage was to have the full machinery of sanctions unleashed against it, each signatory co-operating 'loyally and effectively . . . in the degree which its geographical position and its particular situation as regards armaments allow', under the general supervision of the council.

At the League assembly meeting early in October 1924, forty-eight states received the protocol, without a dissentient, and Henderson welcomed it warmly for the British. The only note even of hesitation was sounded by the Canadian delegate, who compared the protocol to a fire insurance scheme and added: 'We live in a fire-proof house, far from inflammable materials.' But the London press was occupied with a baseless fable that under the scheme control of the royal navy would pass to foreigners; and the internationalist labour cabinet fell a few weeks afterwards.

It is far from certain whether even they could have accepted the protocol as it stood, in view of the grave doubts about its wisdom held in the dominions. Though these states were fully independent, they shared a navy as well as a monarch with Great Britain: that is to say, their own small navies were coast defence forces, quite incompetent to guard their communications with Europe and the mother country. And the naval aspect of the protocol was to this extent alarming, that British ships might find themselves used to interfere with trade between an aggressor state and the USA—which the Americans made it clear, behind the scenes, they would be quick to resent. No one seems to have noticed that this difficulty was just as likely to arise (as in fact it did, later) if the League declared sanctions under its existing constitution.

In any case, the fate of the protocol was soon decided by the new conservative government. Baldwin, not disapproving of the League but not much interested in foreign affairs, was prime minister; the foreign secretary was Joseph Chamberlain's son Austen, a financier-politician who knew little of Europe, and a sentimentalist much devoted to the empire. He might, with better luck, have been prime minister himself—he had led his party for a time, but had been one of the abler conservatives who had tried to stand by Lloyd George when the coalition broke up. Most of these now rejoined the rest; the cabinet's numbers, swollen by lesser men who had dug themselves in in 1923, rose to twenty-one.

Armed with the cabinet's approval, Chamberlain went to Geneva in March 1925 to explain that the British government disapproved the protocol, both on a number of telling points of detail (provided by Balfour), and because they disliked 'the idea that the vital business of the League is not so much to promote friendly co-operation and reasoned harmony in the management of international affairs as to preserve peace by organizing war, and, it may be, war on the largest scale.' In that case, of course, an earlier government in which Chamberlain had also served should never have joined the League at all; but as he said a few days later in parliament, 'I profoundly distrust logic when applied to politics'. His speech at Geneva killed the protocol: without British or American support it could not work, and the states which had already accepted it had to agree to its demise. The League's historian has remarked with justice that, if Chamberlain and his colleagues had been more ready in 1925 to risk a war in some distant spot—the Polish frontier, say?—with scores of

G

allies in the League, it is unlikely that his brother would have
found himself fourteen years later compelled to pledge the country
to fight with no other ally but a weakened and bewildered
France.

Yet though Chamberlain was not an admirer of the League
and its system, he had some sense of history (he had followed,
indeed, an old Foreign Office tradition in resisting compulsory
arbitration) ; and he was anxious to live up to the great traditions
of his new post. He wanted to promote peace ; he saw that the key
to it, for the time being, lay in Germany ; and he welcomed what
appeared to be a German initiative for a general western European
reconciliation. This was to be achieved at a conference to which,
by contrast with the hectic conferences of the Lloyd George
period, months of careful preparation were devoted ; it was held
at Locarno in Switzerland in October 1925, and Chamberlain was
delighted when its conclusions were initialled on his sixty-second
birthday. That there were any conclusions was due partly to sound
preparation, and partly to the readiness of Stresemann the
German foreign minister, who had been a vehement annexationist
during the war, to co-operate for the time being with his French
opposite number, the magnetic orator Briand.

The most important document prepared at Locarno was a
treaty by which Belgium, France, and Germany all promised to
respect their frontiers with each other, and the Rhineland demilitarized zone ; Great Britain and Italy added their joint and
several guarantees of this promise, binding themselves 'immediately to come to the help' of any of the three powers if it was
attacked by either of the others. A clause specifically excepted the
dominions and India from any obligation under this treaty, unless
their governments chose to accept it—which none of them did.
This was a strong guarantee. Its signature was received in London
with extravagant satisfaction, and Chamberlain was made a
Knight of the Garter. But it did no real good ; for three reasons.

Firstly, as the Russians were quick to notice, the guarantee
only applied to Germany's western frontiers. Czechs and Poles
had been at Locarno, and had taken away with them arbitration
treaties with Germany ; yet, though these differed but little from
guarantees against aggression in wording, they were well known

to be of far less diplomatic weight. The implication seemed only too clear : as far as the British and French were concerned, though the Germans must not turn west they could do what they liked in the east. It is true that both Poland and Czechoslovakia already had treaties of alliance with France, and Germany an understanding with Russia ; but these were weakened, not strengthened, by a Franco-German *rapprochement*. Bad as the communists' foreign information often was, they must have realized what anyone who understood anything of Germany knew : that the Germans regarded their frontier with Poland as the least acceptable part of the Paris territorial settlement, and that the old ambitions of the German second empire for expansion eastward were dormant, not dead. The Locarno pact was therefore regarded in Moscow as aimed, ultimately, at Russia ; and it is not surprising that references to 'a new Locarno' by British statesmen, made since Stalin's death, have been coldly received there.

The second point against Locarno was comparatively small, but telling. Though special and distinct military obligations had been undertaken by the British, no directions at all were given to the service departments about carrying them out ; in other words, the cabinet was neglecting a point which meant little to its head and to most of its members—the vital connexion between policy and strategy.

Third, and most important, much of the content of this 'new departure' was not new at all : all the signatories of all the pacts, except Germany, had already by signing the covenant of the League of Nations given a promise that they would not attack each other ; they all agreed that Germany should now join the League ; and the plainest and wisest course would have been simply to arrange for this, without making the various new treaties with their invidious implications.

The moment happened to be one at which the League's reputation stood quite high. Just after the Locarno conference, though before the treaties were formally signed in London in December, it scored its greatest single success : it stopped a frontier scuffle between Greece and Bulgaria from turning into a war. Bulgaria appealed to the League council when fighting began ; Briand, its acting president, telegraphed to exhort both sides to cease firing ; the council met in Paris, and ordered both sides to withdraw; this was done, and the Greeks, who had been rather the more to blame, agreed to pay the Bulgars a small indemnity. In this little triumph the League behaved just as its founders had wanted it to do; it gave both sides a hearing, and it did stop a threatened war. Luck was on its side, because it was Briand's turn to be in the chair, and he was one of its ardent well-wishers; and still more because the dispute was neither between great powers, nor out of the range of great fleets.

Germany's entry into the League was delayed by two hitches. The first article of the covenant provided that each prospective member should 'give effective guarantees of its sincere intention to observe its international obligations', phrases which stuck in the Germans' throats, for they disliked every reminder that they had to pay reparations; and moreover, neither had they carried out all the stages of disarmament to which the Versailles treaty had condemned them, nor had they any intention of doing so; they kept on the nucleus of their forbidden general staff, for example, disguised as the transport section of their war office. The British and French knew quite well that German disarmament was incomplete, and agreed to hush the matter up.

The second obstacle was still more tiresome. Germany wanted to enter the League, and her sponsors wanted her to enter it, as a mark that she was once more being received as an equal among the great powers. Therefore, she must have a permanent seat on the League council. But three powers high in the second rank—Brazil, Poland, and Spain—each claimed the same distinction; and two others, China and Belgium, put in claims for themselves if any of these three should succeed. Chamberlain seems to have supported the Polish and Spanish claims; there was even more bustle in the Genevan hotel corridors than usual at the March meeting of the assembly, and an excessive amount of intrigue behind the scenes. In the end Germany's entry had to be put off until September. She got her permanent seat on the council, but three more temporary seats had to be added as well, to pacify various groups of complainants, and Brazil withdrew from the League altogether.

For the rest of the twenties France and Germany continued, on the whole, to pursue conciliatory policies towards each other;

and Chamberlain could look at some more distant problems. In 1927, in accordance with his party's wishes, he broke off diplomatic relations with Russia, on rather slender grounds provided by a raid on the Russian trading headquarters in London. He wrestled long and unsuccessfully with Egypt's ambitions for independence, which he was not able to satisfy. In China he brought off one stroke he thought useful, at the end of 1926: he displayed a sympathetic attitude to the campaign against foreign concessions of the young Chiang Kai-shek's nationalist movement, the Kuomintang. This strengthened Chiang's hand against the communists by whom his movement was interpenetrated, and the Chinese communist party was broken up for the time being, to the advantage of British traders.

Chamberlain was able to conduct his policies without any interference from Baldwin, with whom his prickly temper had led him to have several quarrels before he went to the Foreign Office; though his own health broke down under pressure of work, and for much of 1928 he was away ill, leaving the office to Cushendun, a dogged Ulster tory, his parliamentary under-secretary. Baldwin, not an energetic leader, was a firm adherent of the *laissez aller* doctrine as far as his colleagues were concerned; and a bemused torpidity settled on the cabinet, enabling its few men of decision to take what steps they wanted without much trouble from their colleagues, except where two of them happened to cross each other's path. Such a clash did arise between Churchill and Amery, Amery pressing for more spending on the colonial empire, and Churchill (who was chancellor of the exchequer, having changed sides again) pressing for less spending on everything. The continued weakening of the navy was also Churchill's responsibility, in that he insisted on rigid economy from all the service departments. At the time, on the advice Chamberlain could give about the improbability of war, Churchill's decision was no doubt fully justifiable; had he chosen the other way, and had the foundations of peace been durable, he would have been blamed for martial extravagance. His later record protects him from the charge of carelessness about defence.

In fact the peace was built on sand. Many ardent peace-lovers joined in the search for some formula that would make future wars impossible, a search that led to so many draft treaties that the French began to talk of the disease of *pactomanie*. The shortest, the most celebrated, the most widely welcomed, and the most useless of these documents was the Kellogg-Briand pact of Paris, to which all the great powers, and almost all the others, adhered in 1928–29. In less than eighty words, its signatories bound themselves never again to use war as an instrument of national policy, and to settle all disputes with other countries by peaceful means. This pact was warmly welcomed by 'world opinion', especially in Great Britain and the USA ; but it was taken not to exclude war 'in self-defence', and the Foreign Office added a characteristic qualification to the British signature, that 'there are certain regions of the world the welfare and integrity of which constitute a special and vital interest for our peace and safety'. Egypt was meant ; but the phrase would equally cover Afghanistan or Persia, or even Belgium. The pledge was of no value, for as the world soon learned it would be evaded by evil men with whose ambitions it clashed ; and its American origins and its brevity kept it from including provisions for any kind of action to enforce it. These provisions indeed existed already in the covenant of the League ; but the carefully chosen terms of that document were less and less regarded.

The great weakness of all the treaties, draft and signed, of this period was that they repeated each other too much ; every new specific pledge threw doubt on the authenticity of the pledges, specific or general, that had gone before. And the world in which this welter of promises was being made was still, in spite of article viii of the covenant, well armed.

It was partly the labour party's enthusiasm for disarmament that secured it a limited success in the general election of May 1929, the first in which all women, as well as all men, over twenty-one could vote. Labour won more seats than any other party, but still had no majority in the commons, fifty-nine liberals being returned to hold the balance ; and moreover labour secured 300,000 less votes, though twenty-six more seats, than the conservatives. MacDonald formed a second government without real power. This time he let Henderson be foreign secretary, and Henderson pursued his usual policy of friendliness. When the government took over, negociations were in progress for a new and more permanent reparations settlement, named after another

American expert the Young plan, to replace the temporary Dawes arrangement. This scheme provided for German payments to be made, on easier terms than before, through a new international bank, up to 1988; dogged persistence by Snowden, the new chancellor of the exchequer, secured for the British a larger share of these payments than the financiers had proposed. Henderson, simultaneously, arranged with Stresemann for the British army of occupation to be withdrawn from the Rhineland by the end of 1929; the French followed next year, five years earlier than the term foreseen at Versailles. Henderson also re-established relations with Russia; but his main interest lay in forwarding disarmament, and to that subject we must now turn.

The League's members were all bound to reduce their armaments; and no project attracted more enthusiasm, all the world over, in the twelve years after the war. Yet though the word 'disarmament' was everywhere spoken with respect, and received the warmest popular support, the act of disarmament was almost everywhere postponed. The British and the Americans fell back quickly, it is true, to a level of arms somewhere near what they had maintained before the war—the British indeed fell back farther, having no German fleet to keep ahead of; and the defeated nations were forced by the terms of their surrenders to fall back a good deal farther still. But an obstinate reluctance was shewn by service departments everywhere to tackle the full obligation in article viii of the covenant. Some of the technical objections that were raised against making a plan for world disarmament were valid, but none were insuperable, given goodwill: what proved insuperable was suspicion. Until it was reasonably sure that it would not be attacked, no state wanted to give up its means of defence. Security and disarmament were not two problems, but two sides of the same problem: till security seemed to be achieved, disarmament had to wait; and when would security even seem to be achieved?

On the naval side, progress was comparatively swift; partly because warships are far simpler to compare than are land and air weapons, but still more because the two leading naval powers, Great Britain and the United States, were not political rivals. Even the naval settlement achieved, under Balfour's guidance, at the Washington conference in the winter of 1921–22 would have been unattainable without a political settlement that had to be negociated alongside it. Under American and Canadian pressure, the British gave up their long-standing treaty of alliance with Japan; and all the powers of the Pacific agreed that they would build no more naval bases in it, nor strengthen the ones they had already. Once this was arranged, fleet strengths could be adjusted, and the proportion of 5 : 5 : 3 was accepted for the principal ships of the American the British and the Japanese navies. It was sensible of the British to accept parity with the Americans, who could by now outreach them in potential building strength; yet the date of the treaty, 6 February 1922, deserves to be noted. It was a milestone on the road down hill.

The British public accepted the decision calmly, for it shared with the British Foreign Office the sure conviction that there could be no war with the USA. But American opinion was much less certain that there could be no war with Great Britain: Irish-Americans and German-Americans were powerful and hostile groups, and could still count on support from millions who bore lasting resentment for British oppressions far in the past. Obstinacy in both admiralties spoiled an attempt to agree about cruisers at Geneva in 1927. A naval conference in London in 1930 did better—future battleship building was reduced on both sides of the Atlantic, and cruiser strengths were adjusted by the three principal sea powers; but the French and the Italians, who had each been accorded at Washington a third of British naval strength, still could not come to an agreement, Italy claiming parity with France and France insisting on superiority over Italy.

Land and air armaments had proved a great deal less easy to adjust. A simple plan put forward in 1922 by that knowledgeable busybody Lord Esher for treating armies like navies, dividing them into blocks of 30,000 men of which each state was to have so many, broke down at once: 30,000 fully trained regulars were clearly not comparable with 30,000 newly enlisted clerks and ploughboys. For a time the diplomats, and the League officials, let the subject drop, while they pursued the search for security. When the Locarno agreements seemed to have achieved this, the League set up at the end of 1925 a 'preparatory commission' to work over the subject; Germany, Russia, and the USA, though none of them at that time League members, were asked to attend its meetings. The Germans early began to air what they regarded as the intolerable grievance that their armaments were limited by the peace treaty, while their conquerors, who had promised to limit theirs as well, did not keep their word. The Russians, struggling desperately to make a socialist economy work, proposed in 1927 that all armies and air forces should be disbanded, and all navies broken up : this would help their economy even more than everyone else's, but of course they did not put this forward as a reason. The only point on which the preparatory commission came near reaching unanimity was when it rejected out of hand this proposal, which ought to have been the goal of all its work. This rejection illustrates vividly both the profound suspicion of revolutionary Russia common at the time, and the reluctance of many countries' representatives to face the realities that lay behind catchwords as popular as 'disarmament'.

Eventually, in 1930, the League was persuaded by Henderson and by the dominions to hold a world conference on disarmament ; sixty-one states were represented at it when eventually it assembled at Geneva in February 1932, and Arthur Henderson was in the chair, though he had ceased to be a secretary of state, or even a member of parliament. It achieved nothing. Fears and jealousies between the member states were far too strong, for lack of any trusted system of security ; the delegates uttered platitudes that seemed to carry no conviction, and were unable to agree even on paper barriers to hold off dangers of conflict that became more vivid even while the conference was sitting. Its very first meeting was held up for an hour while the League's council met to consider the troubles of China.

It was unlucky in its time of meeting : the world was in the trough of the gravest economic depression it has ever had to endure. In the countries advanced enough to publish unemployment statistics alone, over thirty million men were at one time out of work ; even in Russia, fairly isolated from the world market, the slump coincided with the disaster of forced collectivization of the land, in which over a million people died of starvation. No one knew what to do ; and every country sought to protect itself against neighbours and competitors. Tariff walls grew taller, and every one felt less inclined to be generous. A series of European banking catastrophes in the summer of 1931 ruined Austria and Germany, put a summary end to all reparations payments, and threatened even the bank of England. Snowden apart, no member of the labour government—not even Sidney Webb—understood anything of international finance; baffled by circumstances, rated in the press, and daily losing more of the confidence of the country, the cabinet was persuaded to resign by MacDonald at the end of August. MacDonald, taking Snowden and two lesser colleagues with him, entered into a coalition with the conservatives and the less ardently free-trading liberals; under the name of 'the national government', the new cabinet agreed to abandon the gold standard in September, which eased the monetary crisis, and won in the following month the biggest electoral victory in British parliamentary history. 556 coalitionists (including 472 conservatives) faced a few independent liberals and a labour opposition reduced to 46: only one labour cabinet minister, the pacifist Lansbury, survived the deluge that swept all his colleagues out of parliament. The conservatives swiftly took advantage of their dominant position to get what had now become their pet economic panacea, a tariff, enacted; a nominal liberal, Runciman, introduced the first bill in November. An imperial conference in Ottawa next summer provided an extravagant pastiche of the sort of empire tariff programme Joseph Chamberlain had had in mind thirty years before: a formidable barricade of duties, intended to foster the trade of the British empire at the expense of that of the rest of the world. The chief builder of the new system was Chamberlain's second son, Austen's half-brother Neville, who had come late and reluctant to national from local politics ('I grind my teeth', he wrote in 1917,* 'and think if it hadn't been for my d——d well-meaning brother I might still have been Lord Mayor of Birmingham, practically in control of the town'). He was chancellor of the exchequer, and much the most forceful man in the national government; but crabbed and narrow in his outlook on politics, which he seemed always to see through blinkers, looking down the vistas open to an unimaginative midland business man and not seeking to look outside them.

Lloyd George was ill during the cabinet crisis of 1931, and unable to take a place in the new government; in any case (like

* In a letter to his sister of 21 October, deploring his work in London.

Churchill, who was also excluded), he was a firm free trader. A lawyer friend of Lloyd George's, Lord Reading, was MacDonald's first choice for foreign secretary; he had sailed before the mast as a ship's boy, and had later risen to be an eminent lawyer, a viceroy of India, and a marquess; but he had turned seventy, and was settling down to be an elder statesman. The work at the Foreign Office was too stiff for him; and after the election MacDonald dropped him, without remembering to tell him that he was to go. Reading had planned a badly needed expansion of the economic side of the Foreign Office, which his successor dropped; his main actual contribution to British foreign policy was to choose as the parliamentary under-secretary a young MP who had been Austen Chamberlain's parliamentary private secretary: Anthony Eden.

For nearly four years the Foreign Office was in the hands of another lawyer, Simon. Intellectually he was the superior of everyone but Balfour among twentieth-century foreign secretaries; but his career shewed that the driving power of great intellect, without the rudder of full consideration of consequences and a chart of sound principles, cannot make a satisfactory course in foreign policy.

CHAPTER VII

DANGER

1931–1936

SIMON had to consider at once a situation of extreme gravity which had arisen in the far east, the worst political crisis—and the first in which a great power had used force—since 1923. But the far east was far away; the outlook on the world of its statesmen and its peoples was utterly unfamiliar to Europeans, who found themselves faced on every far eastern problem with many uncertainties and few known facts. One known fact was that the Chinese constituted a great potential market; another was that the intensely nationalistic Japanese meant to corner it themselves if they could; beyond that lay the dark. Little was known of the Japanese, save that they were tough; as they were also anti-German and anti-bolshevik, they were believed to be reliable. A clause in the Washington treaty of 1922 had directed a standstill in the building of naval bases in the Pacific; the effect of this was to make the Japanese impregnable to naval attack, and to put them on their honour not to take advantage of the fact. Trust in them turned out ill-placed: having given their word, they broke it, and embarked on the occupation of Manchuria.

Their motives were mixed. First came intense pride, and assurance of the dominating destiny of Japan. Next came economic necessity: without facilities for working Manchurian ores on the spot, Japan could not get the secure base for her heavy industry which she regarded as her right as a great power; lastly, the unemployment crisis caused by a severe American tariff on silk (itself precipitated by the 'great depression') threw hundreds of thousands of Japanese silk-growers into the army; and the army insisted that its swollen forces should not be left idle.

The precise timing of the Manchurian explosion was probably influenced by a passive mutiny affecting five capital ships in the British fleet at Invergordon, whose crews refused duty on 15 September 1931 in protest against cuts in their pay, part of the new national government's economy campaign. No doubt affected by exaggerated reports of unrest in the largest navy in the League of Nations, the Japanese decided that the time for action had come: on the night of 18–19 September a carefully staged explosion at Mukden provided the excuse for a Japanese invasion of Manchuria. Though this invasion was inexcusable in a signatory of the League covenant and of the Kellogg pact, there were some justifications for Japanese claims. Much of China was in anarchy; and the Chinese government was unable to exercise authority enough in its northern provinces to secure to Japan her rights under an exceedingly complicated group of treaties. There was just enough plausibility in the excuses of the Japanese for their high-handed action to baffle and confuse opinion in the world outside China; and they had chosen the moment for their aggression with care. Every country that might be expected to raise objections—except China, which was powerless—was obsessed with the difficulties brought on by the economic crisis: the British, for example, were wholly preoccupied with the danger to the pound sterling, and news from the far east was overshadowed by the country's departure on 21 September from the gold standard. This devaluation attracted far more British attention than was given to Manchuria.

As a matter of fact, nothing could in any case be done to check the Japanese advance. The Japanese would only give way to force, and no force could be brought against them. Practically, the Chinese had none. The Russians remembered defeats in Manchuria a generation before; such troops as they had were most of them at the other end of the trans-Siberian railway; their government, never friendly to the League of Nations (to which Russia did not belong till 1934), was wholly preoccupied with the agricultural disasters of the Ukraine. So there could be no intervention by land; and there could be none by sea either, because there were no naval bases at all within striking range.

Both the powers with navies capable of dealing with Japan's were caught up in the economic whirlpool; and since one was in the League and one was not, co-operation between them was hampered from the start. In fact (contrary to the popular legend) the British and the Americans did work amicably together in the diplomatic field. But the American authorities were determined not to be drawn into any risk of actual conflict, and confined themselves, with legal correctness if with some timidity, to a refusal to recognize the puppet state set up by the Japanese in Manchuria in March 1932.

Legend also has it that men in the Foreign Office who hated the League, using Simon as their willing tool, deliberately seized the occasion to weaken the League and make it look ridiculous. This, again, is untrue. Yet Simon did carry the courtesies of debate rather far at Geneva in the direction of politeness towards the power he should have been opposing; besides, he was a lawyer and approached the problem as a legal one. From that aspect, it was fantastically tangled, and right was not quite clearly on one side. Had he taken, as most of his critics did, the moral line of approach, everything would have looked much more simple, for Japan was clearly in the wrong. But even taking a high moral line, nothing could be done that would have any effect on the Japanese. Even economic sanctions would hardly affect Japan, once she had lost the silk trade with America, if she was going to be able to take over the China market for herself; and in the trough of the depression, League members did not wish to incur the loss of such exports as they made to Japan. Moreover, some account had to be taken of Japan's claims to be in the right. So the League fell back on that drear expedient of baffled politicians, a commission of inquiry. This took a year to report; and by the autumn of 1932 the fact of the Japanese conquest of Manchuria had been accomplished.

The whole affair had been a disaster for the League. By bad luck, its system of collective security had been first seriously challenged in a way that it was powerless to resist; once it had failed a member in a crisis, all its members' confidence was shaken in its ability to sustain any of them as it had been meant to do. Ardent League supporters continued to talk of the security that memberships of the League conferred; but what they said began to ring like the words of the courtiers who admired the emperor's clothes.

The British national government was formed in 1931 to deal with a financial crisis that hardly any of its members really understood. Runciman, a bank director, and Hoare, of a banking family, could no doubt grasp what was going on; Snowden and Neville Chamberlain had worked in this field; the prime minister was at a loss. Snowden resigned, with some other free traders, in September 1932; and thereafter Chamberlain's influence was dominant in the economic field. With him as chancellor of the exchequer, the treasury exercised great power; and this was used, as Keynes's theories of employment had not yet been evolved, to save money, rather than to spend it, throughout the government machine. Necessarily, therefore, armament spending was kept low; a large navy, a small army, and a smaller air force were held adequate to preserve British interests in time of peace, and nothing was done to expand them in view of the new menace from Japan. Research on new weapons was not much encouraged, and general policy rested on the assumption that there would be no major war for ten years at least.

This was an assumption that came naturally to a cabinet mainly composed of elderly men who had hated every minute of the great war: they could not bend their minds with any ease to the possibility that another might ever break out. Indeed, few of them could bend their minds in new directions at all. The younger men, the Raymond Asquiths and Julian Grenfells who should have been coming to the fore in politics, had been killed in the war, or so sickened by it that they had turned away, the whole 'lost generation', from politics altogether. 'Happy are these who lose imagination', said the greatest poet among them, who was killed in the last days of the war; but Wilfred Owen wrote of life in the trenches, not in Downing Street. Nothing is more necessary for a successful foreign policy than imagination; and it was a quality the leading men in this government conspicuously lacked.

In this lack they were not alone. An unimaginative general public cared little about foreigners; was mainly concerned by the need for a revival of trade; and did not seriously consider another great war as possible. Complete pacifism for the first time began to attract a sizeable number of supporters; a pacifist labour candidate won a striking success at a by-election at Fulham in October 1933, winning what had seemed to be a safe conservative seat by nearly 5000 votes. The main influence on the result was probably a local one, for his opponent was a slum landlord; but outside Fulham it was seen as a pacifist victory. This made a considerable impact on leading conservatives, particularly on Baldwin, who became the effective head of the government so far as it had one, as MacDonald's powers began to fail; they believed it to be a sign that pacifist feeling was widespread in the country, and that they should take particular care to keep clear of any troubles abroad.

A similar impression was made by a much-misunderstood inquiry conducted in the winter of 1934–35 by the League of Nations Union. Over 11m people completed a questionnaire circulated by the union, but its results were hard to interpret. Many of those who signed it were under 21; most of them were presumably people favourable to the League. The name given to the inquiry, 'the peace ballot', itself implied a connexion with pacific sentiment. Not much weight should have attached to the very large majorities in favour of continued British membership of the League, and of disarmament; for the questions concerned had been so framed that it was hard to vote the other way. It was more interesting that, in the key question on military action by League powers to support League decisions, such action was approved by only two to one; Cecil, the patron of the inquiry, rightly concluded there was much work still to be done by the LNU in explaining the logic of the covenant to the British people. More careless politicians decided that the ballot shewed public determination to carry out the obligations of the covenant to be weak, and pacifist feeling to be strong.

What meanwhile was happening abroad?

Of the great powers, the USA was emerging from the worst of the depression, remaining isolated, and embarking on the liberal experiment of Roosevelt's 'New Deal'; Japan was consolidating her gains in Manchuria; France, less affected than most other countries by the slump at first, began to feel its effects keenly in the winter of 1933–34. In Germany, which had been hit harder and earlier, a further collapse of the currency combined with massive unemployment to produce a political disaster. The nazis—the best organized, the richest, and the most hectic of the German extremist parties—had become more and more prominent since 1930; on 30 January 1933 their leader Adolf Hitler became chancellor of Germany. In March he secured, by various dis-

honest devices, a fairly subservient parliament, which passed an
enabling act giving him legal authority to do whatever he chose.

This evil and dangerous fanatic was also, unhappily, a man
of subtlety; and so plausible were the accounts of his steward-
ship that he gave to the world outside Germany—and, indeed,
to the imperceptive German public—that it took people years to
realize how evil and how dangerous he and his followers were.
With passionate verbosity, the nazis poured out abuse of the
Diktat of Versailles, babbled of the superiority of German culture
and the purity of the German race, and hinted—not obscurely—
that they meant to fulfil the old nationalist slogan, 'Germany is
ours today, the world is ours tomorrow'. In fact their regime, for
all the talk of culture and purity, was barbarous and corrupt. The
armed thugs of the party terrorized the cities; all other parties
were abolished; the press, the churches, the universities were
gagged; one of the main motive forces of the leaders was sadism,
vicious delight in the spectacle of suffering. The nazi programme
was devoid of any real content, save a lust for power for its own
sake. As a shrewd observer commented, too late, their revolution
was a revolution about nothing at all. Its apostles talked much of
honour, but did not respect it; boundless bad faith was the outstanding characteristic of the movement. This made the nazis
dangerous neighbours; though the English, at least, were slow
indeed to realize the fact.

A weaker version of the same mixture had been applied in fascist Italy for years: reverence for a single leader, gifted with powers
of bombastic oratory and supported by a numerous private army
of toughs and gangsters; ardent xenophobia, coupled with ardent
claims for colonial expansion; no reverence for law, and only
such order as suited the leader's wishes. These were often violent.
Fascism believes, said an article signed by Mussolini in 1932,
'neither in the possibility nor in the utility of perpetual peace. . . .
War alone brings up to its highest tension all human energy, and
stamps with the seal of nobility the peoples that have the courage
to face it.' He had only been able to seize power because not even
a few men of resolution had been among his opponents in 1922;
and the frivolous and the absurd continued to play a part in
Italian politics. Italian schoolchildren, for example, began their
day's lessons by chanting ten fascist commandments, one of

H

which proclaimed that 'Mussolini is always right'. The fascists felt that Italy had not done as well as she should have done out of the peace settlement, and pursued a policy of unashamed self-aggrandisement, up to the limit of Italy's resources. These were not large, but they did include an efficient aluminium industry, and with the help of this the Italians secured for a time, in the middle thirties, the fastest and most powerful air force in the world.

The remaining country of serious military capacity, Russia, was still strong rather in population than in that industrial power which provides, in the present century, the index of greatness. After Lenin's death in 1924 the communist leaders had fallen out among themselves; Trotsky, the most brilliant of them, had been elbowed out of the way by a superficially much duller character, Stalin, who by skilful manipulation of the party machine eventually secured supremacy for himself. In 1928 Stalin launched Russia on its fourth modern revolution, intended to industrialize the country properly for the first time, and so raise it to the level of greatness of Great Britain or the USA. His ultimate aim, of course, was to spread communism over the whole world; he believed that a strong socialist Russia was a necessary first step. Though the very name of Russia had been abandoned by the diplomats of the Union of Soviet Socialist Republics, Stalin's slogan of 'socialism in one country' admitted the fact. The task he set his adopted country (he was himself a Georgian, not a Russian) was too vast for even his abilities as an organizer to carry through fast or smoothly. Success came in the end. But the price included, as well as much bureaucratic confusion and the farming catastrophe of 1931, an extraordinary police operation that began at the end of 1934 and involved, in the course of the next three or four years, the arrest of several million people, including a substantial proportion of the new managerial class and nearly all the senior officers of the armed services. Surprisingly little was known about this great purge outside Russia. It coincided with one of the not infrequent sharp turns in Russian foreign policy, this time away from denunciation of non-communist left-wingers as 'social chauvinists' towards 'popular fronts' of all parties hostile to the capitalist Establishment, a policy which captured the enthusiasm of many radicals who

would have been appalled had they known then what was actually
going on in the country whose system they praised.

The strategic effect of the purge was to make Russia unfit to
take part in any major war for several years : a point not missed
in staff planning circles, either in London or in Rome or Berlin.

This then was the background to British foreign policy in the
middle thirties. The habit of co-operation with France, re-
established at Locarno, was on the whole continued, though the
two countries were not linked by any important treaty—except
the League covenant. The British indeed distrusted the elaborate
system of alliances by which the French had associated themselves
with the states that had succeeded to the outlying provinces of the
defunct Habsburg monarchy, and preferred to keep their hands
as free as they could.

Yet the Foreign Office remembered an elementary principle once laid down for diplomats by Bismarck : in a world
dominated by five great powers, always be one of three. Ignoring
the two great powers outside Europe (for nothing could be done
about Japan, and the USA was busy with its own affairs), the
Foreign Office looked at the continent, and decided that friendly
relations were desirable with another great power besides France.
Anti-German feeling was strong enough for the choice to lie
between Italy and Russia. Russia was unacceptable for a number
of reasons, principally the total lack of confidence on both sides.
Given that Europe was still to be run on Bismarckian lines, there
was no alternative to the attempt to detach Italy—or rather,
Mussolini : the dictator could speak for the country—from the
camp of revisionist powers. This scheme was foredoomed to
failure because all Mussolini's long-term interests lay, as he came
to realize, with Hitler, in favour of a re-drawing of the map of
Europe and Africa to suit them both. In any case, did the premise
on which the attempt was based still hold ? The peace settlement
had blurred the old distinction between great powers and small ;
and the League of Nations offered a new form of European organization, the grand design of collective security—all powers, great,
small, and middling alike, banded together against an aggressor—
which was meant to stop exactly the type of febrile expansionism
for which Hitler and Mussolini stood.

But when it came to the pinch, the British government was not ready to stand by the covenant of the League, or by the arrangements made with the League's blessing at Locarno. The main reason for an attitude that seems in retrospect so short-sighted was fear—fear first of an Italy, and then of a Germany, that seemed to have grown too strong for limited British arma-ments to match them; and fear combined with humanitarian reluctance to risk any war, and lack of faith in the ability of the collective security system to prevent a large war by sustaining, if necessary, a small one.

The year when Germany broke the Locarno treaty, 1936, is usually looked back on today as the worst, the fatal year of 'the twenty years' truce'. But the really disastrous year was 1935; for that was when Germany remade the army without which she would never have dared to flout Locarno, and when the League system, which alone could have checked even a re-made German army in time, was ruined by the Italian adventure in Africa.

Ever since Hitler had come to power, the nazis had been busy with the work of rearmament in various fields. Having disposed of enemies in and near his own party by several score assassina-tions in midsummer 1934, and seen his domestic programme well on the way towards abolishing unemployment by putting the unemployed to make arms, Hitler proclaimed in March 1935 that Germany was no longer bound by the disarmament clauses of the Versailles treaty, already had an air force, and was forming an army of thirty-six divisions. The admiralty knew also that she was building two battleships.

Hitler accompanied this announcement, in a manner that was to grow familiar, with lavish promises of goodwill and recon-ciliation once others recognized Germany's right to equality in arms. Simon and Eden had already arranged to visit him; they thought it rude to put their journey off, but in Berlin they could do nothing but see, and regret, the armed men who had sprung from the dragons' teeth sown by German nationalists since the war. Simon was told, falsely, that the German air force was already as large as the British. 'Agree with thine adversary quickly, whiles thou art in the way with him' seems to have been the text upper-most in British minds; for the government concluded a treaty with Germany in June which allowed the Germans a third of British naval surface strength, and eventual equality in submarines. This selfish arrangement gave great offence to the French, whose navy had been limited by the Washington treaty to the same size that the British now conceded unilaterally to Germany.

In April a joint Anglo-Franco-Italian conference had been held at Stresa, in the Italian lakes; the British and French tried to get Italian co-operation against the visibly reviving menace of Germany. Mussolini was glad, rather than sorry, to see the German threat to France re-born, for he had been busy for eighteen months with plans in another quarter. It was well known that a quarrel was pending between Italy and Ethiopia; nothing was said about it by the British or the French at Stresa, though they had brought experts competent to discuss it; Mussolini concluded that they would not oppose him, and on 3 October his armies crossed the Ethiopian frontier.

Next month Baldwin, who had succeeded MacDonald as prime minister in June, held a general election, on a programme of moderate rearmament and strong support for the League.* The conservatives' vast majority fell, but they still had a comfortable one of nearly 250; the labour opposition and its allies counted 159, and there were a score of opposition liberals.

The election took place, of course, in the midst of the crisis that arose from Mussolini's aggression. Hoare, Baldwin's new foreign secretary, made a brave speech at Geneva in September about the virtues of collective security; but his heart was not in strong action to prevent Mussolini from doing what he liked. Germany was already too frighteningly strong for the British chiefs of staff to look with any relish on the prospect of diverting forces to a Mediterranean war; and British opinion had not accepted Litvinov's paradox that to preserve peace it is sometimes necessary to fight for it. So British policy was founded on the premise that no risk of war with Italy must be run. French policy worked from the same fatal assumption; Mussolini perceived

* It is still sometimes held that Baldwin confessed to the commons in November 1936 that at this election he deliberately misled the public about his party's intention to re-arm. So far as any definite implications can be found in his rather confused speech, it appears that he was not referring to the actual election of 1935, but to a possible general election (never in fact held), which was contemplated for some time in the winter of 1933–34.

that his bluff would not be called,* and hastened his advance in Africa.

In the previous year, Mussolini had taken strong exception to a German threat to Austria, when Viennese nazis murdered the Austrian chancellor Dollfuss. Relying on this transient attitude, the French government still cherished the already obsolete hope that Mussolini would join in opposing German expansion, if Italy's expansion was not hindered. In December the French foreign minister, the odious Laval, persuaded Hoare to agree to a plan by which Italy could keep those parts of Ethiopia she had already conquered, with an economic monopoly over much of the rest of the country, in exchange for the cession of a small port to the Ethiopians. News of this proposal leaked into the French press, before it had been put formally before either Mussolini or the League.†

Strong resentment was at once expressed by all parties in England, in an outburst so vigorous that the cabinet hastily withdrew the provisional sanction it had given to Hoare's proposal. Hoare still thought the plan a good one; so he had to resign. Eden, lately admitted to the cabinet in the new post of 'minister without portfolio for League of Nations affairs', succeeded him at the Foreign Office. But there could be no real change of policy, since the chiefs of staff for military, and the cabinet for political, reasons did not dare to face the chance of war. The Mediterranean fleet, confident in its superiority, was ready to fight; but the admiralty, alarmed at Italian air strength, forbade it to take any risks. It was felt that any sign of vigorous British opposition to Italy would provoke Mussolini into a 'mad dog act', a sudden onslaught on some precious British possession; so nothing vigorous was done.

The League covenant's article xvi laid down in some detail the steps which its members were to take in severing all relations, political, economic, and personal, with any member state that attacked another. No one could doubt that Italy had attacked Ethiopia; but the full sanctions authorized by the covenant did

* His secret service had access at that time to the files of the British embassy in Rome.

† Baldwin later believed, on the evidence of friends in Italy, that Mussolini might have originated the plan himself.

not follow. Obsessed by fears of an immediate Italian attack which in fact they could easily have repelled, and of an eventual German attack against which they mistakenly hoped for Italy's aid, the British and French governments led the other members of the League, with gingerly hesitation, to apply just enough sanctions to annoy the Italians irretrievably, but not enough to help Ethiopia by making any serious difference to the Italian war effort. Diplomatic relations with Italy were unbroken; and tourist traffic, an important source of foreign exchange for the Italians, was not interrupted. Either of two measures could have stopped the war at once: the closing of the Suez canal, or an embargo on the supply of petrol to Italy. No government proposed the closing of the canal, which was in any case illegal; though this might have been the moment, natural justice might have provided the reason, and the international court might have provided the channel, for making new law. The petrol embargo (called the 'oil sanction') was also not applied; several US oil companies were making money out of selling petrol to Italy, and fear of American resentment was too strong. (Roumanian petrol exports to Italy also increased.) So Mussolini's armies went ahead, and by a lavish use of air bombing and poison gas quickly overcame Ethiopian resistance.

Its failure to protect Ethiopia was fatal to the League. No one could any longer have any confidence in its system of collective security; every one was thrown back on

> the good old rule . . . the simple plan,
> That they should take, who have the power,
> And they should keep who can.

Its institutions at Geneva remained in existence; its subsidiary organs went on doing such useful work as improving labour conditions and reducing the traffic in drugs; but the heart had been taken out of it, and no one counted on it for safety any more.

In this harsh new world the British found themselves with extensive commitments, and inadequate resources to carry them out. Lack of arms dictated the ineptitudes of British policy towards an Italy that had feared the royal navy till air power came to redress the balance at sea. Slowly, reluctantly, and in advance of public opinion, the government began the task of setting the nation's defences in order. Ironically enough, MacDonald's initials appeared in March 1935, not long before he ceased to be prime minister, on a white paper which expounded the need for the country to re-arm. Two decisions which turned out later to have been of vital importance were indeed taken in 1935—to produce the Spitfire fighter, and to establish in great secrecy a chain of radio-location posts round the coast. But the processes of rearmament were painfully slow, as the aggressive powers well knew; and knowing when they were going to attack, they could make sure their own forces were properly equipped before they began. In Great Britain, the three service departments competed wastefully, and Neville Chamberlain kept tight hold on money. In March 1936 Baldwin at last appointed a minister for the co-ordination of defence. Churchill was the man clearly fitted for the task; Hoare ardently desired it. Baldwin chose instead a politically inconspicuous lawyer, Inskip, for whose nomination a quip of Mr. Gladstone's was revived: 'The most surprising public appointment since Caligula made his horse a consul'.

March 1936 is more famous for a coup that Hitler executed on the seventh—a day chosen with care: it was a Saturday, and he rightly assumed that British ministers would have dispersed into the country before news reached them that the new German army had re-occupied the Rhineland zone which Germany was pledged to leave without troops. The pledge, first given at Versailles, had been specifically renewed at Locarno, and re-affirmed by Hitler as lately as May 1935; its violation was declared by the main Locarno treaty to be a cause for war.

It is now known that the German occupying troops were under orders to withdraw if they encountered any serious armed resistance; but they met none. The thirty-six divisions of the 1935 programme still existed mainly on paper, and the available strength of the armies of France, Czechoslovakia, and Poland was ninety divisions. Not unreasonably, the German generals— and indeed most of the nazi leaders—were seriously perturbed when they got the order to march. But Hitler had gauged with devastating accuracy the timidity of his opponents. No action was taken to force Germany to keep her word. The Poles urged invasion on their French allies; but the French would not stir without the British, and the British, aware of their own unreadiness, fell back on the comfortable remark, 'After all, isn't he simply walking into his own back garden?'

This success for Hitler fortified his self-confidence, which had always been immense, and much encouraged those near him to trust his judgement in future. The German public, already heartened by the end of unemployment and disciplined by a ruthlessly efficient security service, was elated at a step that asserted Germany's independence of her detested conquerors, and was content to accept Hitler's lying explanation that he had not really broken the treaty of Locarno because it had already been destroyed by a treaty of mutual assistance lately ratified between France and Russia.

Opinion gradually began to swing against the nazi movement in the countries of western Europe. Not much was known about German home policy; little was revealed, in a popular press anxious to entertain its readers, about the concentration camps that had been started in 1933, or about the virulent anti-semitic policy which they helped to carry through; and the serious newspapers were more concerned at the brutalities of the nazi attitude towards the churches. Yet the stridency of German claims for expansion was noticed, and it began to be clear that the new German army was not intended solely for ceremonial purposes; though curiously little heed was given to the calling up of two classes for it instead of one in the autumn of 1936, a step that clearly presaged trouble in the autumn of 1938.

Feeling for and against the dictatorial regimes in Europe was brought into focus by the fighting that broke out in Spain in July 1936. What had been intended as a sudden *coup d'état* by the group of generals who led it turned instead into a bitter civil war. The generals had been assured of German and Italian support before they raised their revolt; indeed some Italian troops arrived in Spanish Morocco before it began. Italy and Germany were anxious to embarrass France and Great Britain by securing a regime in Spain friendly to themselves; but the French and British governments alike were as blind that summer to the strategic dangers of a hostile Spain as they had been blind that spring to the strategic dangers of a fortified Rhineland.

To most Englishmen there could be no doubt that right was on the side of the republican government of Spain. Eden, for one, saw the struggle as simply one of right against wrong; but he could not carry the cabinet with him. The record of each side was stained by savage atrocities. The British cabinet, seeing black marks on both sides, determined on complete neutrality, and brought effective pressure on a French government similar in complexion to the Spanish to adopt the same course. Reference to the League being by now regarded in London as practically useless, the British organized a non-intervention committee. All its members promised not to send men or arms to Spain, but only the British and French governments kept their promises. Germany and Italy sent large contingents from their air forces to fight on the generals' side; the Italians also sent several divisions of troops and many submarines. For the republic, the Russians sent a very few excellent fighter aircraft (without spares) and a number of technical advisers and police; and the communist parties of western Europe and the USA collected an efficient international brigade.

Non-intervention, in fact, was a farce, despised and neglected by Hitler and Mussolini, who paid lip-service to it, yet soon staked their prestige on the generals' victory by recognizing Franco's regime at Burgos as the legitimate government of Spain. Had Franco been prevented from getting German and Italian help, he would certainly have been beaten by the unaided resources of the Spanish republic; as it was, the republicans had to endure air attacks against which the British and French would not even allow them to purchase purely defensive artillery, and were eventually borne down by sheer weight of numbers and equipment.*

The British attitude towards the war in Spain, inglorious though it was, was at least prudent. General opinion was badly muddled by various and contradictory reports, which aroused

---

* One curious by-product of this dismal war deserves to be noted. For once, German staff officers made a mistake: they made wrong deductions from experience in Spain about the kind of bomber aircraft that would be needed in a modern war. The Germans in 1940 were equipped with bombers that had a defensive armament quite inadequate to repel British eight-gun fighters. The British, more sensibly, developed a medium bomber with an effective sting in its tail, a four-gun power turret.

religious and political antagonisms. Among politicians, labour MPs strongly supported the Spanish republicans, with whose ideals they sympathized; the conservatives were divided. Many of them distrusted the communists in the republican government, and exaggerated their influence; a few were deeply exercised at the prospect of Italian control over the western Mediterranean. Many more, especially among those in office, were alarmed at the prospect of war, and ready to sacrifice much to avoid any risk of it.

These timid and peaceable men found a leader after their own hearts when Baldwin retired in May 1937 and Neville Chamberlain succeeded him.

CHAPTER VIII

THE FRUITS OF APPEASEMENT

1937–1940

BALDWIN, knowing little of the problems of the continent, had never had a foreign policy of his own. Chamberlain was hardly more knowledgeable; but he was self-reliant to the point of conceit, and thought himself capable not only of understanding, but of solving, those problems that Baldwin had neglected. He repeated Lloyd George's cardinal mistake in the field of foreign policy: the two sides of Downing Street began again to speak with different voices. Chamberlain relied largely for advice on Sir Horace Wilson, an eminent treasury official who knew as little of the continent as himself; and on the two former foreign secretaries in his cabinet, Simon and Hoare—neither of them a conspicuous success in that post. With Eden, nearly thirty years his junior, he was never temperamentally in accord; and he mistrusted such expert advice as the Foreign Office could give.

Through his brother Austen's widow, he approached Mussolini in July 1937, and tried to establish an Anglo-Italian entente. He was checked for a moment by the success of a conference held at Nyon, a few miles outside Geneva, in September, which Eden attended and he did not. Eden persuaded the French to agree that their two navies should sink any submarines they could catch in the international waters of the Mediterranean; and a brief display of resolute activity produced results at once. Piratical Italian sinkings of merchant ships of many nationalities ceased abruptly.

Eden was anxious to press on from this naval success to secure a substantial reduction in Italian help for Franco by land as well, and tried to make Chamberlain insist on appropriate clauses in the projected Anglo-Italian agreement. But Chamberlain was determined to do nothing more that might annoy Mussolini, and Eden, finding no support in cabinet, realized that no course was left him but to resign. One might say that nothing in his conduct of the Foreign Office, through two unfortunate years, became him like the leaving of it in February 1938. His under-secretary, Salisbury's grandson Cranborne, resigned with him, and was replaced by R. A. Butler. But they were both too keenly aware of the dangers of the world situation to be anxious to press their recent colleagues hard in parliament, which was a mistake, as it left parliament and the public alike inadequately informed.

To the labour party's annoyance, Halifax the new foreign secretary was in the lords. He was both distinguished, as a former viceroy of India, and a figure to inspire confidence. He had committed one indiscretion, when he had told Hitler in November 1937 that the nazis had performed a service to Europe by acting as a bulwark against communism; but this was kept secret for years, and his promotion added almost as much weight to the government as Eden's departure had taken from it. He by no means wholly concurred in his prime minister's policy of a friendly attitude towards the great dictators. Indeed study of the Foreign Office documents since published indicates that he and Chamberlain were not seldom at cross purposes, but Chamberlain remained master, and simply overruled Halifax when necessary to suit his own purposes of appeasement.

Hitler by now was taking up the running from Mussolini. On 5 November 1937, a fortnight before he saw Halifax, he proposed to a conference of his service chiefs the expansion of Germany, in the near future to absorb Austria and Czecho-slovakia, and ultimately much farther. His soldiers were worried at the strength of the Czech fortifications; he relied himself on his belief that 'in all probability England and perhaps also France, have already silently written off Czechoslovakia, and that they have got used to the idea that this question would one day be cleaned up by Germany.'

Barely conscious of the venomous jealousy with which Hitler regarded the British empire, Chamberlain continued his policy of making concessions to those who asked for them. Early in 1938 he engaged in talks with the Irish, which resulted in the giving up by the British of the three naval bases retained under the treaty of 1921. This surrender was unnecessary, for the Irish did not really expect it, and had only put the demand forward for the sake of driving a good bargain later on ; moreover, it was perilous in the extreme, given the Anglo-German war that was by now a probability. A few years later it increased the toll of merchant seamen, and the intense danger to Great Britain's food supplies, from German submarines. However, Chamberlain's supporters welcomed it at the time as a proof of good intentions.

While Chamberlain was busied with this significant capitulation, and with his talks with Mussolini, that bore only Dead Sea fruit, Hitler was pressing on with his November programme. In February he threatened Austria, and next month his forces overran it ; it was declared an integral part of the German state. A few hundreds of its Jewish inhabitants escaped ; many committed suicide ; many more were rounded up in concentration camps, and many of these were ultimately murdered. The nazi ministers, who were already briskly competing with each other for administrative empires, moved in to consolidate the conquest.

This *Anschluss* between Germany and Austria was of course yet another breach of the treaty of Versailles, as well as a breach of numerous personal assurances by Hitler, some only a few weeks old : but nobody dared do more than wag a finger in protest. The British appeasers had counted, up to the last moment, on the Italian attitude remaining that of four years earlier, when Dollfuss had been murdered ; but Mussolini was by now bound by treaty to Germany, and inclined by Italian self-interest to stand by what a treaty said. In November 1937 he had joined the year-old pact between Germany and Japan, aimed actually at the power that lay between them, Russia, though nominally at the communist international, the Russian-dominated committee in charge of the foreign policy of communist parties the world over. This was the moment when Mussolini finally decided to enter Hitler's camp ; Chamberlain had nothing to offer him that would make him change his mind. So the Italian earned the lasting gratitude of the German dictator by accepting the disappearance of Austria without protest.

There was nothing the British could do. The French prime and foreign ministers, Daladier and Bonnet, came to London a few weeks later, to discuss how the two powers might concert future action ; and were told that the available British expeditionary force would consist of two divisions, incompletely equipped. The thought of this heartened them little when Hitler opened his diplomatic batteries against his next target, France's ally Czechoslovakia, where there was a large German minority.

Most of the German minority dwelt near the mountains of Bohemia, within a frontier that had not changed since the xii century, on lands that had never been governed from Berlin. They were probably the most generously treated minority population in Europe, with full democratic political, as well as religious and cultural, rights. But Hitler had long before asserted the principle laid down in the *Rolliad*:

> How clear, convincing, eloquent, and bold
> The bare-faced lie, with manly vigour told;
> Which, spoke in public, falls with greater force,
> And, heard by hundreds, is believed of course.

He had put this principle into his intolerably tedious book, *Mein Kampf*, written in prison in 1924. Unfortunately, no full English translation of it appeared till the summer of 1939; and there is no evidence that any British minister waded through it in German. With the help of the most efficient propaganda machine in the world, he poured out a torrent of lies, deftly mixed with half-truths and an occasional truth, to the effect that the Germans in Czechoslovakia were being persecuted, and longed to come under nazi rule. Very considerable force, ranged since the *Anschluss* round three sides of Bohemia, visibly backed up his claim.

Chamberlain, mistrusting as usual the diplomatic machinery available to him, sent Runciman to Prague to look into this problem; he chose a man likely to tell him what he wanted to hear. Runciman paid full attention to the Germans' claims, with which he found himself in sympathy; but had to admit in the end that the intransigence of the nazi extremists among them prevented the home rule settlement he had at first favoured, and recommended the transfer of the German-populated areas to Germany.

This solution had a certain appeal in Great Britain; it had been put forward by the *New Statesman*, and then (more or less accidentally) by *The Times*, before ever Hitler officially made it his own proposal. There were over 3m German speakers in Czechoslovakia, and to leave them under alien rule seemed to contradict the principle of self-determination for which the great war had been fought. The political and strategic dangers that would accompany the transfer were little regarded; and the solution of the problem that was ultimately adopted in 1945— forcible mass deportation of the Sudeten Germans over the mountains—was ruled out of court in 1938, by Hitler because he wanted more territory, and by everybody else on grounds of common humanity.

Most of the opponents of the 1938 settlement of the Czech question have described it as a clear choice for the British cabinet, which past British eminence forced into the lead, between maintaining or handing over to nazi domination the only genuine democracy in Europe (save Sweden) east of Switzerland. But the choice that presented itself to the prime minister was as usual a choice of two evils, not a choice between evil and good. The dominions, long hesitant about European commitments of any kind, made it clear that for them the Czech imbroglio was what Chamberlain called it in a broadcast on 27 September, in a phrase unforgivable in a British prime minister, 'a quarrel in a far-away country between people of whom we know nothing'; and that if the British cared to go to war about it, they would have to do so without Canadian, or Australian, or South African help. Given Hitler's evident determination to fight, sooner than recede from his demands on Prague, the choice therefore was not between preserving and destroying the Czech democracy, but between preserving the Czech democracy and preserving the unity of the empire. It was a choice that a son of Joseph Chamberlain could only make in one way.

Besides, the prime minister was perfectly sincere when (in the same broadcast) he spoke of himself as 'a man of peace to the depths of my soul': humanity, not cowardice, made him shrink from war. He knew the weaknesses of British armaments; they largely stemmed from his own policies as chancellor of the exchequer. He had little confidence in France, and none in Russia: it may even be that the anxious care the Russians displayed for Czechoslovakia's integrity helped to prejudice him against that unhappy republic. Whether Russian support for the Czechs would have gone to the point of war in 1938, and whether, if so, the Russian armed forces could have acquitted themselves with credit at a moment when most of their trained staff officers were in prison, are interesting but unanswerable questions.* What is certain is Chamberlain's profound mistrust of the communist government of Russia.

When Hitler's demands on the Czech president Beneš became so strident, in September 1938, that an explosion seemed imminent, Chamberlain put himself forward as a mediator. With more courage than judgement, he undertook three journeys to Germany by air to see what he could arrange by talking to Hitler face to face. The results of these meetings may be given in Churchill's summary to the commons: '£1 was demanded at the pistol's point. When it was given, £2 were demanded at the pistol's point. Finally, the dictator consented to take £1 17s. 6d. and the rest in promises of goodwill for the future.'

The outcome was bad enough for Czechoslovakia: a meeting at Munich on 29-30 September of Hitler, Mussolini, Chamberlain, and Daladier decided that German troops should enter some of the Sudeten areas on the day Hitler had long fixed for the invasion —1 October—and the rest in the following ten days. As he left London for Munich, Chamberlain quoted Hotspur to the crowd: 'Out of this nettle danger, we pluck this flower safety.' He should have remembered how the passage goes on: 'The purpose you undertake is dangerous, the friends you have named uncertain, the time itself unsorted, and your whole plot too light, for the counterpoise of so great an opposition.'† Inconclusive arrangements were made for a guarantee to what remained of Czechoslovakia. The Czechs were forbidden to destroy any installations as they withdrew: this meant the surrender, intact, to Germany of a most powerful belt of concrete fortifications, designed on the same plan as the main frontier defences of France (the Maginot line), of which the secrets were thus revealed. Yet the manner of the Munich settlement was hardly less endurable than the matter

* There is much evidence to suggest the sincerity of Russian support for Czechoslovakia in the autumn of 1938, but hardly any to indicate how the Russians would have overcome Polish and Roumanian objections to the transit of Russian troops or aircraft across their territories, which lay between Russia and Czechoslovakia.

† *I Henry IV*, II, iii.

of it. Beneš was not represented at the meeting : as Seton-Watson put it, the Czechs 'could not be offered a chair at the conference table, because they were to be strapped down for vivisection on the table itself'. The Czech envoys who went there were arrested at the airfield by the secret state police (Gestapo), who held them *incomunicado* for some hours. In the small hours of 30 September Chamberlain—'constantly yawning, without the least sign of embarrassment'—and Daladier met them, presented them with the terms already signed, and made it clear that the only alternative to acceptance was war with Germany, in which Czechoslovakia would get no British or French support.

Details were left to an ambassadors' committee, sitting in Berlin : a Czech representative was required to attend by 5 p.m. that day. Beneš gave way. He could not bear to plunge his country into a futile war, and accepted humiliation for the time being, with a hope that in the end truth would prevail. Next day he accepted another ultimatum, this time from Poland, moving in for a share of the spoil; then he resigned, and emigrated to England. Almost without exception, the ambassadors' committee decided doubtful points in Germany's favour ; and the rump of Czechoslovakia was left to maintain itself as best it could.

Hitler was not really satisfied with the Munich settlement ; by now he was beginning to thirst for more violent action. Another dictator was much put out by it. Stalin was mortified that the great power of Russia had been treated as in eclipse, and not invited to attend. The excuse Chamberlain gave, that there had been no time, had a grain of truth in it, so hurried had been the arrangements for the conference, which he described as 'the last desperate snatch at the last tuft of grass on the very verge of the precipice'.* Ever since the Anglo-German naval treaty of 1935 the Russians had doubted whether the British could really be relied on to oppose nazi expansion ; the timid British attitude in the Spanish war, in which Russian sympathies were warmly engaged on the republican side, had reinforced the doubt ; Munich confirmed it. Thereafter Stalin began to look out for a chance to make a temporary accommodation with Hitler.

For the moment, though, it seemed in Whitehall that the means

* In a letter to his sister, written on 2 October, just after his return from the ordeal of the conference.

for effective opposition to Germany simply did not exist. Most of the navy's ships were obsolescent. The army was tiny. The radar chain had hardly been begun. Worst perhaps of all, in September 1938 only a single squadron (twelve aircraft) of modern fighters was capable of firing its guns above 15,000 feet (this was due to an unhappy fault in design, modified out in the coming winter). So how could war be risked, now that past follies had made ineffective the League that had been meant to make disarmament safe?

Yet during that terrible month war was, for the first time for twenty years, impressed on the minds of everybody in Great Britain as an imminent possibility. There was visible activity to meet it on every hand. The fleet was mobilized on 28 September; the territorial anti-aircraft units had been mobilized already (though they had exceedingly few guns of adequate range). In every city, trench air-raid shelters were dug in the parks; volunteers delivered gas masks to every house.

There was immense relief when it turned out at the end of the month that there was not to be an immediate war after all. It is common form today to vilify the Munich agreement and its makers; but it should not be forgotten that the overwhelming public reaction to it at the time was one of thankfulness. Nevertheless, it ought never to have been necessary to sign it; and the memory of the policy that led to it still keeps many Englishmen away from the party of Neville Chamberlain. At the time, only one member of his cabinet resigned—Duff Cooper, one of the youngest men in it; himself a former diplomat, and a friend of Churchill and Eden, he alone among his colleagues thought the casting of Czechoslovakia to the wolves so dishonourable that he could take no share in it.

On the morrow of the Munich conference Chamberlain suddenly signed with Hitler a formula of his own devising. He had the legal adviser of the Foreign Office with him, but referred to this draft as his own. He had taken to Munich none of the senior Foreign Office personalities; Wilson, as inexperienced as himself in the ways of diplomacy, accompanied him instead. His formula spoke of 'the desire of our two peoples never to go to war with one another again', and 'resolved that the method of consultation shall be the method adopted to deal with any other

questions that may concern them'. This of course meant nothing
to Hitler; but the prime minister treasured it, thought it meant
'peace in our time', and cherished the hope that all would yet be
well.

He was rudely awakened six months later. Hitler had in his
usual style proclaimed the Sudetenland to be his 'last territorial
demand in Europe'; as usual, he did not mean what he said.
With the 'lightning swiftness' he had laid down as necessary in
November 1937, he overran the remnant of Czechoslovakia in
March 1939.

No immediate step was taken by the British to restore the
vanished state. Inskip had told the commons in the previous
October that the government 'feel under a moral obligation to
Czechoslovakia to treat the guarantee as being now in force'; but
the technical diplomatic moves to complete it had never been
carried through. As far back as June 1938 the Foreign Office had
been hunting for 'some face-saving and, if possible, also effective
device' for such a guarantee; but neither before nor after Munich
had a formula satisfactory to all the powers concerned been
found. Yet now, with some pressure from Halifax, Chamberlain abruptly shifted his line in foreign policy. He could no longer
conceal from himself the true character of the man with whom he
had to deal. Hitler had done something which at once stung
Chamberlain's vanity, and presented itself in terms with which as
a business man he was thoroughly familiar: the German dictator
had made a contract, and then broken it. There were also powerful reasons of policy for the change, that public opinion approved.
Till now Hitler's gains had all been justifiable, more or less,
on some ground or other of national self-determination; but
such arguments could not apply to the latest act, an act of naked
aggression in search of the *Lebensraum* the nazis had long and
ardently demanded. Clearly the time had come for the other
European countries to call a halt to nazi expansion—if they
could.

Absolutely speaking, the British armament position improved
substantially in the year that followed Munich: the expeditionary
force was doubled, the radar chain was extended from Hull to
Dorset, some excellent fighter aircraft became available, and

heavy anti-aircraft guns began to come forward. Inskip was replaced in February by Chatfield, an experienced sailor; in April, a ministry of supply was at last set up to organize the production of warlike stores. But this same year of absolute increases was a year of relative decrease with regard to Germany—the German superiority in armaments, especially in tanks, got still larger. The fine Czech army, thirty-six divisions strong, was no longer available against Hitler; and the famous Skoda munition works was now producing for him.

Nevertheless, Chamberlain had reached the sticking point; and by now he could carry most of the country with him in proposals intended to bring Germany to a halt. Mistrust of him was still lively enough in the labour party for its members to oppose his introduction of peacetime conscription, in May; trade unionists and politicians alike feared so powerful a weapon in his hands. Before that bill was passed, the revolution in foreign policy was complete. A guarantee was given to Poland that, if Germany attacked her, she would receive British support; she had been promised French aid since 1921. When on Good Friday Mussolini seized Albania, similar British guarantees were given to Greece and to Roumania: the first signs that Chamberlain was abandoning the policy of friendship with Italy. No doubt he did so because Mussolini, also, had broken his contract: in the Anglo-Italian agreement of Easter 1938 he had promised to effect no change in the Mediterranean without prior agreement with London, and no warning had been given of his Albanian adventure. Covenants without the sword are 'but words and breath', as Hobbes remarked; but the sword was being forged and the will to wield it was there.

Meanwhile Hitler, pursuing his programme with his usual assurance, turned his attention to Poland as soon as the Poles had refused an offer to join him against Russia, and he had cleared his right flank by taking Slovakia. The German minority in Poland, even on the Polish estimate, was over a million strong; though its members were not particularly well disposed towards the excesses of Hitler's Germany, they had not been well treated by the Poles, and numerous incidents were provoked by nazi sympathizers in the corridor of Polish territory that cut Germany in two, and also in the German city of Danzig, administered under

League auspices on its coast. Through the summer of 1939 the stream of nazi invective against the Poles grew into a torrent. On 11 August Mussolini's young son-in-law and foreign minister, Ciano, met Hitler's foreign minister Ribbentrop at a country house near Salzburg. As they took a turn in the garden before dinner, 'Well, Ribbentrop,' asked Ciano, 'what do you want? The Corridor or Danzig?' 'Not that any more,' Ribbentrop answered casually, with a stony glance; 'we want war.'

What could be done to attack, or to defend, Poland hinged on the attitude of her eastern neighbour, Russia; and during that summer the British, carrying the French with them, embarked reluctantly on negociations for Russian support. They were far from anxious for success. Chamberlain's unadventurous mind, prejudiced against Russia from the start by the distrust of communism that was almost universal in British business circles and among the squirearchy, had been set in its prejudices by the secret service reports he saw, which indicated communist hostility to Great Britain to be as uncompromising as ever. As early as 18 March the British made their first advances towards the Russians; but the Russians made many difficulties, and their counter-proposals were coolly received. Neither side was, in fact, really anxious to close with the other; and Stalin was playing a double game. Just before the German conquest of Czechoslovakia, on 10 March, he threw out a hint in a speech that he would welcome better relations with Germany; and the Germans took the matter up quietly through their diplomats. They could offer Stalin what the British and French could not, a share in Poland itself; and the British and French had placed themselves under a further tactical disadvantage by saying that they would support Poland whatever happened, before ever they opened detailed talks with Russia.

For Hitler, as for Stalin, it was not easy to turn back on fifteen years' denunciation of the kind of regime the other headed; and each must have known that the other hated him, and in the end only desired his downfall. But each had his country firmly insulated from contact with the outside world; each had an efficient propaganda machine; each looked, for the time being, only to the short run. Hitler wanted to conquer Poland; Stalin wanted time. They came to an arrangement; on the night of 23-24

August Ribbentrop signed a pact of 'friendship' with Russia in Moscow. A secret appendix envisaged the division between them of the intervening states.

Therein, as Namier has pointed out, lay such responsibility as rests on Stalin for the outbreak of fighting; for Hitler took the conclusion of this pact as the signal to start his war. A last-minute message from Chamberlain persuaded him to delay his offensive for a week, which he devoted to a specious attempt to persuade the British not to honour their guarantee. His final excuse for action was provided by an attack on a German broadcasting station at Gleiwitz, several miles inside the Silesian border; the attackers wore Polish uniforms, but they were Germans under sentence of death, and their uniforms had been provided by the German secret service. Ribbentrop galloped insincerely through the forms of a diplomatic protest, without giving the Poles any real chance to enter negociations, and early on 1 September German forces began the conquest of Poland.

The British had begun to mobilize as soon as it was known (on 21 August) that the Russo-German pact was imminent; the obligation to fight in Poland's defence was perfectly clear, and as perfectly well known in Berlin as in London. To the sharp annoyance of the house of commons and of the public, the declaration of war was delayed. The reason for the delay, which could not be published, was that the French government was making difficulties: it was prepared to close with a proposal of Mussolini's for another conference, without setting any conditions about a pause in hostilities. Mussolini, not best pleased at Hitler's agreement with Stalin, pleaded the inadequacy of Italy's armaments, and stayed neutral for the time being.

Eventually, the British declared war on Germany on the morning of 3 September 1939; the French followed suit that evening. All but one of the dominions, finally convinced of the need to extirpate nazism, entered the war, Canada, the latest of them, on 11 September. Ireland remained neutral.

'There can hardly ever', as Churchill wrote afterwards, 'have been a war more easy to prevent'—had the task of preventing it been undertaken early enough, and had the genuinely peace-loving powers been ready to pay the price of preventing it: a possible cheap and short war to prevent one certain to be long and costly. This time there were none of the interminable disputes about the responsibility for the origins of the war that have engaged so many publicists and scholars since 1914: the main burden lay so obviously upon one man, Adolf Hitler, and upon his intolerable demands. Yet though the verdict of history against him is clearly one of 'Guilty', it is not possible to acquit everyone else: some blame does attach itself to many millions of people. It falls primarily on Hitler's henchmen in the nazi party, and on the German people who welcomed nazi power. But some part of it falls also on the statesmen and the peoples, all the world over, who—whether from ignorance, from self-interest, or simply from indolence—did nothing till it was very nearly too late to check Hitler's Germany in its advance to domination.

Nothing could be done to help Poland, whose armies were swiftly overwhelmed by German land and air forces, working in technically admirable co-operation. On 17 September Russia also invaded Poland, and that country disappeared from the map. The German and Russian security services exchanged, at Brest-Litovsk on their new and common frontier, refugees from each other's despotisms; and the Russians proceeded to strengthen their territorial buffer against Germany by annexing the three helpless Baltic states of Estonia, Latvia, and Lithuania.

Churchill and Eden were at once brought into the government: but labour and liberal distrust of Chamberlain remained keen, and the cabinet remained purely conservative. Four divisions were sent to France, and six more followed during the winter (three of them without artillery). By May 1940 these ten divisions formed a tenth of the French and British land forces; the Germans had 155 divisions under arms. There was practically no fighting, and the British devoted themselves to preparing a defence line along the Franco-Belgian frontier, which the French, with blind trust in the Locarno treaty, had left unprotected by a Maginot line. The cabinet resigned itself to a long war; plans were slowly set on foot for an army of 55 divisions, and for the necessary conversion of the whole national economy to the purposes of war. These measures eventually absorbed the army of unemployed, who had been the standing shame of Great Britain between the wars; there had been over a million of them ever since 1920. Vast arrears in preparation had to be made up; for Hitler had taken full advantage of knowing when he was going to strike, and had all his war production factories ready.

For the time being the British were desperately short of equipment, particularly in the air; so it was as well that air activity also was slight in the first winter of the war. The civilian population had to put up with the lesser discomforts of total war —conscription, anti-aircraft blackout, rationing, and general dislocation of life—without the compensating elation that comes with the visible presence of danger. The country's mood on the whole was dogged, even sullen; the nazis had clearly gone too far, and had got to be stopped—somehow; but the initiative for the time being lay with the enemy, who had the greater strength. Many sincere pacifists, a few outright pro-nazis, and another handful of communists under Moscow's orders, definitely opposed the war; they carried little weight.

Churchill supervised the naval war with vigour. German submarines were active; one of them sank an unescorted Cunarder, the *Athenia*, on the first evening of the war; another got into Scapa Flow and sank a battleship; but the losses in merchant shipping were kept low by convoys. The Germans sent out a few surface raiders, which caused a disproportionate diversion of British capital ships from home waters; they did little actual damage, and one of them, the pocket battleship *von Spee*, cheered the British by scuttling herself in the River Plate in December when cornered by three much more lightly armed and armoured British cruisers. An almost complete blockade of Germany by sea was established; but it could have little economic effect while Germany could draw on the resources of Russia.

Russia meanwhile, pursuing the policy of establishing buffers along her western frontier, tried to make Finland go the way of the other Baltic states. The Finns did not propose to lose their independence without a struggle, which the Russians soon forced on them; for the Finnish frontier lay at one point as near to the centre of Leningrad, the second city of the soviet republic, as Gravesend does to Westminster. The Russians, viewing an eventual German attack, determined to force this frontier at least back to a safer distance, and attacked Finland at the end of November. At first they made little progress; and by their attack, provoked by nothing except strategic considerations, they shocked a great many people. The League, dying quietly of inanition at Geneva, exhibited a last flicker of life in expelling the Russians as covenant-breakers. Chamberlain was so carried away by strength of political prejudice and weakness of strategic judgement that he proposed to the French not merely the supply of scarce arms to Finland, but active help to the Finns by allied ground and air forces. A considerable quantity of arms was in fact sent. Forces, detailed to 'volunteer' in a manner unpleasantly reminiscent of German intervention in Spain, were actually standing by to leave England when the Finns at last, on 12 March 1940, gave in to superior numbers.* The British were thus fortunately saved from a course of action which would probably have been fatal to the liberties of the world.

As the dismal winter of 'twilight war' drew to a close, both sides considered operations in neutral Norway. The Germans struck first, and struck hard: on 9 April, taking Denmark in their stride, they captured the four best ports of Norway, and rapidly took over most of the rest of the country. Superior air power, and a clearer idea of what they were trying to do, enabled them to defeat with comparative ease the allied forces which arrived a week later. The only benefit the allies got from the campaign was that the German surface navy was crippled in a number of small actions with the British.

Sharp dissatisfaction was expressed in London at the failures in Norway; brave men, it was felt, had been sacrificed to little purpose. Hesitation and timidity seemed to have been the ruling passions at a moment that called, as the Germans had shewn, for decision and ruthless daring. These feelings were voiced in the house of commons in two days of furious debate, on 7 and 8 May; on a vote of censure, nearly forty conservative members divided against Chamberlain, and about twice as many abstained. He still had a majority of 81; but his hold on the house was plainly going, and his hold on the country had gone.

Early on 10 May the Germans opened a tremendous onslaught

* Anyone taking the London–Oxford road past Northolt aerodrome that afternoon could see a squadron of RAF Blenheims on which the British markings were being painted in again on top of Finnish ones—blue swastikas on a white ground.

from the air on neutral Holland and Belgium, repeating on a wider scale and with the most up-to-date appliances the devastating right hook against France that had so nearly succeeded in 1914. Chamberlain, with a last flicker of conceit, thought for a moment that everyone would now rally to him, but found he was wrong. In this darkest hour Churchill was called at last to take command.

CHAPTER IX

MORTAL PERIL

1940–1945

THE British nation now became organized for war. Churchill, relishing the vast increase in authority that came with promotion to the leading place, at once assembled a coalition of all parties. He formed a small war cabinet, only five strong at first—himself; Halifax, still at the Foreign Office; Chamberlain; and two labour party leaders, Attlee and Greenwood. He formed a new ministry, of defence, and headed it himself. It absorbed—indeed, it largely consisted of—the staff of the long-standing committee of imperial defence; and undertook, with great efficiency, the central direction of all British operations of war. As in the crisis of 1916, singularly few of the usual difficulties were made by the politicians: the Germans were overwhelming the low countries fast, the emergency was visibly desperate, everyone went where he was told.

Churchill never uttered a word of public reproach in 1940 to the people who had so mismanaged his country's foreign policy, and restricted its armaments, as to leave it in mortal danger when he took over. As he put it forcefully, 'If the present tries to sit in judgement on the past it will lose the future'; he looked only to the future, with a splendid self-confidence that he managed to communicate to his colleagues and to the country. Taught by the disasters of Norway, he realized that the air arm had now become vital, and persuaded Beaverbrook, the owner of the *Daily Express*, to set up another new ministry, of aircraft production. By ferocious, unconventional, and effective wrestling with bureaucrats and manufacturers, Beaverbrook drove up fighter production per month, which had been 35 at the time of Munich, from 325 in May to 490 in July. His energies and abilities secured a seat for him in the war cabinet from August 1940 to February 1942.

By July, all land fighting on the continent had ceased. Holland withstood the German assault for five days, Belgium for eighteen; France for less than forty. The French front was broken open at its hinge, by an attack through the Ardennes, which the French staff had wrongly thought impassable for a large army; tanks poured through the gap made at Sedan, across Picardy, to the sea. The French had, by a staggering error, failed to provide a general reserve; their high command, their government, their army, their people, were sunk in varying degrees of apathy and despair. The BEF, cut off to the north of the German penetration down the Somme valley, tried without success to move southward, and then withdrew, in a fighting retreat, to the beaches by Dunkirk. From these beaches a third of a million men were saved, by a suddenly improvised armada of destroyers, cross-Channel packets, trawlers, yachts, and fishing-smacks; but they had to leave everything behind them that was too heavy to carry in a man's hand. The Germans could have prevented the evacuation; but their army hesitated, and their air force suffered severe casualties in pitched battles with British fighters.

The French begged the British to transfer their fighters to French bases; but the cabinet would not permit the home-based strength in fighter squadrons to fall below twenty-five (300 operational aircraft, with another 300 in forward reserve on the airfields); less would endanger control of the air at home, and thus imperil the nation. Instead, the cabinet offered France an integral union with Great Britain. There was little time to mull over the formidable complexities that would have beset this project, had it gone forward, and none to put it before parliament, let alone the country: it was conceived, in a moment of impassioned generosity, by men conscious of France's plight and anxious to keep her in the war.

The defeatists in the French cabinet, headed by the aged Pétain, would not consider the proposed union; in the third week of June France surrendered, stabbed in the back by an Italian declaration of war just before she fell. At the end of the month the Germans occupied the Channel Islands, which could not be defended against them: this was their only seizure of British territory throughout the war.

A few weeks' pause ensued, invaluable for the British, who

put the island's defences in order, brushing aside a German pro-posal to make peace, and demonstrating their bellicosity by destroying a French fleet at Oran which refused to sail farther away from the Germans. At last, under the spur of imminent danger, everyone began to work. Parliament passed in a day an act which placed everybody, 'themselves, their services and their property at the disposal of His Majesty'. The beaches of the east and south coasts were sown with obstacles; great anti-tank ditches were dug across the ways to London; a volunteer army of amateurs, the Home Guard, grew to a strength of over a million in a few weeks, and was armed with old rifles willingly sold by America. Bevin, minister of labour in the coalition, per-suaded the trade unions to accept longer hours and shorter holidays; production figures in all the war factories soared.

Over a country thus occupied burst in August the series of air engagements, lasting on into October, known as the battle of Britain. The German air force, from its new bases in the low countries and in France, engaged in a protracted and deliberate attempt to destroy the power of the RAF—the necessary pre-liminary to invasion; and it failed. The cabinet's determination in May and June to keep the metropolitan fighter force intact was justified by the results of air fighting from July to October. The few hundred fighter pilots of the RAF fought like tigers, with skill and confidence and daring, ardently supported by their ground staff and by army AA units. The radar chain gave them indispens-able help. The Germans, with slightly faster but slightly less manoeuvrable fighters, had a superiority in numbers of two to one, and had moreover the initiative in places and times of attack; but they lost two aircraft for every one they brought down. Their strategy was faulty: twice they laid their finger on an essential link in the British system of defence, and each time they lifted it before it had pressed hard enough. Had they persevered in their attacks on radar stations, instead of switching to fighter airfields; or had they persevered in their attacks on fighter air-fields, instead of switching to an onslaught on the more easily located target of all London, the result of the battle, and with it the whole course of the future, would have been different. For the battle of Britain, like the battle of the Marne, was decisive: it ensured a long war. The British only just won it; as Wellington said of Waterloo, it was 'a damned nice thing—the nearest run thing you ever saw in your life': but win it they did.

So the Germans could not carry out the operation they had been planning since early July, the invasion of England. The German sailors rightly maintained that they could only carry soldiers across the Channel under an air umbrella: and this umbrella the RAF never allowed the German airmen to put up.

The grand decision in foreign policy made in 1940, the decision to go on fighting after France gave in, was never taken deliberately, or rather it was taken for granted, by everyone concerned. We have Churchill's word for it that the question, as such, never came before the war cabinet. His own courage and determination never wavered for an instant; nor did those of the men he had gathered round him to carry through the programme he put to the Commons in May—'to wage war against a monstrous tyranny . . . victory in spite of all terror, victory, however long and hard the road may be'.

Full public support was given. In the late summer of 1940 the whole British nation was as nearly at one as it has ever been. Comparisons with the year of the armada readily came to mind —there was the same universal feeling of crisis, danger and elation; and there was no equivalent in 1940 to the English catholics of 1588 whose loyalty was not wholly given to the first Elizabeth. Very few pro-nazis indeed were left by September 1940; and the handful of communist sympathizers whose loyalty to their party had survived the shock of seeing its doctrines applied in Finland lay low. Ireland apart, the whole empire agreed with the home country in detesting Hitler and supporting the war; but the dominions and colonies had been even less prepared for war than the United Kingdom, which for many months withstood the Germans and Italians practically alone.

Having failed to secure control of the air by day, the Germans turned to indiscriminate night bombing—first of the giant target of London, which they bombed for 57 successive autumn nights, usually with about 200 aircraft; then of various provincial cities, most of them either centres of arms manufacture or ports. Far less heavy casualties could, at this stage, be inflicted on the Germans after dark than by day, though many surprising diversions of their effort were achieved by small bands of experts who interfered with their methods of guiding their bombers onto the target. But this was not, on the British side, primarily an experts' battle : it was rather a protest by the entire population against an attempt by a foreign power to enforce its will on them. The whole mass of the people, in uniform and out, men, women, and children together, had a sole object : to win the war. Such a spirit is hard to break ; Hitler's Germany had not the weapons to break it. The Londoners, who were bombarded longest, deserve special mention for dogged resilience ; but as Churchill wrote after the war, 'It did not matter where the blow struck, the nation was as sound as the sea is salt.'

German air strategy was no better in the night battle than in the day ; it showed a similar lack of perseverance against particular targets. And Hitler, misreckoning the British as powerless to do him harm—counting them indeed as already beaten—turned his attention elsewhere, while the factories his air force had failed to destroy toiled night and day to forge the weapons that were to bring him down.

Mussolini meanwhile offered little menace. So rapidly do aircraft become obsolete that when his air force, lately so terrible, tried to play a part in the attack on Britain it lost 13 aircraft in a day, inflicted no damage, and did not come again.

The Italian army in Tripoli set out to conquer Egypt ; but the task was far beyond it. It crossed the frontier indeed in September, but then sat down for three months, not daring to move ; and in December a much smaller British force threw it back, not only out of Egypt, but out of all Cyrenaica as well. This force had been equipped in the late summer, thanks to a display of rare courage and judgement by the cabinet, with half the available British tanks ; there were, at that moment, less than 500 all told, and the invasion of England was awaited from week to week.

Great Britain was reaping, in fact, all the advantages in foreign and military policy that come from a strong cabinet under a strong leader, a body that knows what it wants and is ready to take risks to get it. Churchill followed the motto of one of the youngest, but not the least gallant, regiments in the army : 'Who dares, wins'. From his first few weeks in office he began, for example, to press on the building of tank landing craft and the forming of special hunting groups of shock troops, later called commandos; his attitude, in a year spent on the defensive, was based always on the old saw that attack is the best form of defence. The contrast with his three predecessors in his great office was remarkable.

The risk of sending the tanks to Egypt had been well calculated. There turned out to be no need for them at home—rather to the disappointment of some of Churchill's sterner advisers, who would have welcomed a German invasion attempt for the sake of the crushing defeat the Germans would, they believed, have encountered. Whether such an invasion could have been thrown back, had it ever secured a lodgement on an English shore, is another question.

When the tanks got to Egypt, they did useful service; but it was not decisive. For three years to come war ebbed and flowed along the north coast of Africa; a purely professional war, largely conducted over uninhabited desert, of much technical but comparatively slight political interest and importance.

Frustrated in Tripolitania, Mussolini turned to the Balkans, and in October 1940—without telling Hitler he was going to do so—tried to invade Greece from Albania. The Greeks held him up through the winter; but the Germans, coming to the Italians' aid, cut down through Yugoslavia and Bulgaria in the spring, and struck the Greeks in the flank. The British did not forget the guarantee they had given to Greece in the summer of 1939; they sent four RAF squadrons there during the winter, and in April sent an expeditionary force of British, Australian, and New Zealand troops. This was a hard decision to make; it dangerously weakened the desert armies, which now had to face Germans as well as Italians; but the Greeks were determined to fight anyhow, if necessary alone, and the British thought it dishonourable not to stand by their guarantee.

Eden, who had just become foreign secretary again,* went out to Greece with the CIGS, to reconnoitre; and it was on their advice that the cabinet decided to act. But the Germans, working

---

* Halifax, still mistrusted by the labour party as a *munichois*, stepped down in December 1940 to become a highly successful ambassador in the United States. Churchill first offered this post to the seventy-seven-year-old Lloyd George, who rightly concluded that he was too old for it.

on interior lines, could concentrate much more powerful forces; and again an expeditionary force had to be evacuated, at a heavy cost in equipment. Most of the troops were taken to Crete; and this island the Germans conquered in May 1941 by an operation that is, so far, unique: a purely airborne invasion. Attempts to reinforce the Germans by sea were all baffled by the Royal Navy. The Cretan battle, demonstrating the future of air power, presaged a new kind of war. But it tore the heart out of the only German airborne division, and Hitler was never able to make strategic use of his parachutists again.

A still more important result of this German campaign was that it delayed Hitler's next move for several critical weeks. The Russian leaders, with singular folly, made no attempt to frustrate his Balkan advances, ignored the warnings Churchill and Roosevelt sent them of imminent German hostility, and continued to supply Germany with raw materials for making war—as it turned out, war on themselves. Early on 22 June 1941 Hitler launched the last and largest of his surprise attacks at an unprepared foe: his troops and aircraft poured over the frontiers of Russia.

Churchill, than whom the communist government of Russia had known no sterner enemy in its extreme youth, rose to the occasion. In one of his finest wartime broadcasts, made that night, he wiped a sponge over the past, proclaimed Russia's danger to be Britain's too, and offered generous and whole-hearted help to anyone who would join in the effort to stamp out nazism from the face of the earth.

The Russians, a trifle sourly, responded; they let it be known they would be glad of any assistance the British could lend. They were at once engaged on a much wider front, and with much larger forces, than the British could ever hope to emulate; and did not hesitate to plead their losses in men and land as reasons why the British should make every conceivable sacrifice in their support. They were driven back over some five hundred miles in the first three months, Leningrad was besieged, and late in the year German troops caught sight of the turrets of the Kremlin of Moscow.

The British were willing to do what they could; but some obstacles of time and space and material could not be overcome. The Russians never appreciated the complexities of combined operations over sea, and clamoured from the start for the opening of some other front in continental Europe that would relieve the strain on themselves. This, for two years, was simply a technical impossibility: the landing craft, without which it could not be done, did not exist. Moreover, the cabinet was determined to do all it could to help Russia, but felt that seriously to endanger the country's survival was something it could not do; so no extravagant risks were taken.

Popular opinion, refreshed by the thought that another great power had now joined in the war, was enthusiastic in its support for the 'gallant Soviet ally'; and of course the diversion of the main German effort eastward lightened the burden of air attack that had hitherto lain heavy on the people of the British Isles.

Yet the war was still far from won: it had not yet run half its course, and many disasters for the British lay ahead. It seemed indeed, that autumn, as if the worst of all might impend—a quick victory by Hitler over Russia, after which his ever-victorious army would march westward, get into its landing barges, cross the Channel, and conquer Great Britain at last. However, Hitler handled the Russian campaign with a less sure touch than he had displayed in the battle of France, for which he had conceived the break-through in the Ardennes, or in the battle of Crete, where again it was he who proposed the use of the airborne division. In both cases, as earlier, over the Rhineland coup, he had acted against expert advice; so his experts had become shy of advising him. Had he followed the opinion of Halder, his army chief of staff, he would probably have utterly defeated the surviving Russian field forces round Moscow; but instead he plunged his armies south-eastward in search of oil, till the terrors of a Russian winter came upon them.

The balance of forces was restored by the intervention of the United States. Though this did not become fully effective till the Japanese attacked the Americans in December, amity between Roosevelt and Churchill had already combined with warm sympathy felt by millions of Americans for the gallantry, and the sufferings, of their British cousins to produce much effective American assistance to the British war effort. Early in 1941 the Americans began to lend to the British, whose dollar supplies were already running low, substantial quantities of war equipment

—lent, without charge, without question, without 'strings' of any kind, until the war should be over. This same generous system of 'lend-lease' was applied to the Russians too, as soon as they were attacked by Hitler; through it the Russians obtained, eventually, the great fleets of lorries which made their armies largely independent of railways, and these made possible their almost fabulous feats of logistics.

Churchill and Roosevelt met off the coast of Newfoundland in August 1941, and issued the Atlantic Charter, a declaration of principles that favoured self-determination and equal economic opportunities for all nations after the war; it included a reference to 'the final destruction of the nazi tyranny', strong words to come from a supposedly neutral state. By this time, indeed, Roosevelt's America had made it clear by actions as well as words that it was committed to the British side.

The commitment came, as it had done before, from the depredations of German submarines. Churchill confessed, when the war was over, that these, and these alone, had really frightened him among the devices Hitler had deployed against the British: for they threatened starvation, and therefore surrender, if only they could close their grip on the sea routes to the British Isles. As before, they showed little more respect for neutral than for British ships; and they sank about four million tons of shipping in each of 1940 and 1941. The Royal Navy, and a whole command of the RAF, were engaged throughout the war in formidably difficult and complicated tasks of convoy escort and of submarine hunting. These tasks were made more difficult and more complicated by the lack of southern Irish bases; and any relenting or relaxation in them brought mortal danger.

As soon as he became prime minister, Churchill had asked Roosevelt for 50 old American destroyers, obtained in September 1940 in exchange for west Atlantic bases; and in April 1941 the USA began to shadow and report (though not to attack) any submarines it could find throughout the western Atlantic. So by the time Japan forced the USA into actual fighting, the Americans had in fact been actively helping the British for some time.

Japanese ambitions had grown no weaker since 1931, and the moment seemed a good one for steps towards their fulfilment, since all the powers except the USA were engaged at full stretch elsewhere, and America could be struck a staggering blow at the start. Japan's action was precipitated by an embargo which Great Britain and the USA had placed on exports of petrol to her in July; her stocks were limited, and there were oil fields for the seizing in the Dutch East Indies. The Japanese followed in 1941 their precedent of 1904: without pausing to declare war, they attacked the main battle fleet of their intended opponent.* On 7 December 1941 Japanese aircraft crippled the American fleet at Pearl Harbor, Hawaii, sinking four out of eight battleships and heavily damaging three more; three days later, Japanese torpedo bombers caught one of the newest British battleships and a battle cruiser off the coast of Malaya without air escort, and sank both. This made them masters of the Pacific and Indian oceans—for a time.

On 11 December 1941 Hitler and Mussolini, fulfilling a treaty engagement with Japan, declared war on the USA. The declarations spelled doom for them both: thereafter, their end was certain. In the long run Germany could not hope to withstand the vastly greater productive resources of America; Italy, far less. But in the short run, how many others might they carry down with them?

The first months of the war against Japan brought a series of catastrophes for the British in Asia which none could endure without shame, and only the best informed and longest-sighted could endure with any equanimity. Malaya, a vital source of rubber, was easily overrun, and the circumstances of its fall were not creditable to the British as a colonial power. The Japanese moved round into Burma, cut the road by which a few supplies had been passed to the struggling Chinese, raided Ceylon, and threatened India itself; their occupation of Burma precipitated a rice famine in Bengal so severe that some 2m Indians died of starvation.

Early in 1942 Churchill took the advice of the cabinet† and

---

*The excellence of the American deciphering service made available to very restricted circles in London and Washington hints that they were about to go to war a few days before they did so.

† The war cabinet, as reconstructed in February 1942, consisted of Churchill, Eden, Anderson, and Lyttelton for the conservatives, and Attlee, Cripps, and Bevin for labour. Cripps had been Churchill's imaginative choice as ambassador to Russia; but had had to leave after a year, as the Russians found out he had endorsed his military attaché's opinion in June 1941 that the Russian armies would be unable to withstand the Germans for long.

of the principal experts about the policy that should be pursued towards Japan. Provided the Russian front held, it was feasible to stand on the defensive in Asia once difficulties of supply had checked the Japanese advance. The war in the Pacific could then be left to the Americans, who were more keenly interested in the defeat of Japan than in the war in Europe and Africa, while the British stepped up their offensives in the Libyan desert and their air attack against German home territory. In fact, the more expensive decision was made : that offensive war, on as large a scale as possible, was to be waged on Japan, Italy, and Germany at once. It was not, of course, a decision that could be put before the public, or even before parliament, in time of war; though there is little doubt that both would have approved the course taken.

The choice, though glorious, was ruinous as well; for it necessitated a scale of armament so vast as to entail the selling out of the very last reserves of securities abroad that remained. This meant that Great Britain, which had entered the war a considerable creditor, would emerge from it internationally bankrupt, and dependent for some necessities, as well as all luxuries, on the charity of the Americans. It may be taken as marking the end of the island's existence as a very great power.

The first half of 1942 was an uphill struggle for the newly formed and ill-assorted alliance of America, Great Britain, and Russia against Germany. The Russians, reasonably enough, maintained they had too much on hand in Europe to be able to fight in the far east as well, and did not declare war on Japan. They never dropped their guard towards their new allies, volunteering hardly any information about their proposed operations, and maintaining, in a stream of surly messages, insistent demands for equipment of every kind and for the immediate opening of a second front. They managed to hold their own front in being against their late ally, and present enemy, at the cost of further huge sacrifices of south Russian territory.

In 1942 the German submarines had their most successful year of the war; they sank over three million tons of shipping in the first seven months, and sank another three and a half million in the ten months that followed. Most of these successes were won at first in the Caribbean, or close to the American coast; for the Americans were slow to get active anti-submarine measures under weigh. Indeed, the process of mobilizing the USA for war took a long time; and for two and a half of the three and a half years the two were fighting side by side, the British had more troops in actual contact with the enemy than had the Americans.

Some impatience with Churchill's conduct of the war was expressed in 1942 by the London press, and by a couple of dozen left-wing snipers in parliament. The cry was for more vigour, more efficiency, and more imagination; in fact it was not that Churchill was lacking in any of these qualities, but that his critics wanted more success. Some of them may also have been motivated by jealousy of his position, which was unusually predominant for a democratic country. One of his colleagues is said to have described his system graphically as 'dictatorship by monologue—none of us could get a word in edgeways'.

A more serious criticism of Churchill was that he concerned himself too much with the problems of strategy overseas, and too little with organizing the home front. He did not altogether neglect home affairs, but his interventions in that field were erratic, and he did not give the impression of having economic subjects at his finger-tips. He paid for this later.

Military success came late in the autumn, when the tide of the war turned.

The British and the Americans set up in Washington a combined chiefs of staff committee, which directed all the outline planning for the war. With its approval, a combined Anglo-American expedition landed in French north Africa in November 1942, and in six months' hard fighting joined with the British army in the Libyan desert to eradicate, at last, all the German and Italian forces on the south side of the Mediterranean. Alexander co-ordinated the blows from east and west with acute judgement; and took by May 1943, when the chase ended at Tunis, nearly a quarter of a million prisoners—about as many as the Russians secured in their simultaneous encirclement of the German army that tried to capture Stalingrad.

In July and August Sicily was overpowered by another joint

Anglo-American landing, and the allied forces moved on into Italy. Mussolini fell from power, and the Italians changed sides; but the political opportunities provided by this transformation scene were not exploited as fully as they should have been, and the Germans established a fortified line across central Italy which they held without trouble through the winter of 1943–44.*

It may be questioned whether the diplomatic direction of the war was as successful as the strategic. The British constantly reiterated that they had no wish to make terms with Hitler; and had agreed with the Russians in July 1941 not to make any separate peace with him. Roosevelt and Churchill went so far as to announce, eighteen months later, that their countries would fight on till the 'unconditional surrender' of their enemies was achieved. This was intended to guard against any repetition of the misunderstandings between Germany and her conquerors that had helped to befog the Paris peace conference; but its public announcement served to arm the Germans with the courage of despair. The overwhelming might now being collected on the allied side began to attract a few of the remaining neutrals —Portugal, for example, at last allowed the Azores to be used as an anti-submarine base from October 1943, and Spain (whither Churchill had sent Hoare as ambassador in 1940) became less and less accommodating to those who had helped to establish her new regime. Russian armies began their long advance westward. But the decisive crushing of German power remained to be accomplished.

To the already overwhelming technical difficulties of a landing on the coast of north-west Europe was added the shortage of landing craft caused by the Americans' claims for the Pacific, where they were engaged in the reconquest of the islands lost in the first half of 1942. At first, Churchill contemplated an invasion of France in 1943; a good deal of planning was done for it, but neither the landing craft, nor the troops, nor the necessary air superiority were available in time. Eventually, an enormous armada was landed on the coast of Normandy on 6

* Mussolini was rescued from captivity in south Italy by a brilliant raid by German airborne troops, and set up the ghost of a fascist regime in the German-occupied north; when the front in Italy finally crumbled in April 1945 he made for Switzerland, but was caught and shot by communist partisans.

June 1944. The defenders, taken by surprise, were stunned by naval gunfire and an overwhelming weight of air attack.* The landing area had few ports of its own; but artificial ones ('Mulberries') were created with concrete piers, a pet idea of Churchill's dating from the previous war, and fortunately omitted from his memoirs of it.

The Germans remained convinced for some weeks that the Normandy landing was only a feint, and that the real thrust would shortly come on the beaches south of Boulogne. This was not so. But it took six weeks' severe fighting in the Norman hedgerows to get clear of the landing area. After another month of struggle thereabout, the Germans' front broke, and American and British armoured divisions chased them back to the Rhine, where shortage of petrol brought a check. After the war, German generals said that if the British had pressed harder against their right wing, after capturing Brussels, they would probably have broken through to the Ruhr and brought the war to an end there and then. But the British forces on this front, which had been as large as the American in June, were already inferior to them in numbers; by May 1945 there were three American soldiers in this theatre for every one British. All came under Eisenhower the American supreme commander, who fought his war in the lavish American fashion, pushing forward on a broad front instead of concentrating on one or two deep thrusts. The delay he imposed on the British advance gave an instance of the way in which, as they developed their superior power, the Americans became, from the British point of view, more and more intractable, and paid less and less attention to British advice or requirements.

The allied armies' advance across France and Belgium could be made along the main roads. The villages, and whole provinces of west and south-west France, were liberated by the bravest of

* Several months earlier the German embassy in Turkey had provided hints (ignored in Berlin) about the impending landing, deduced from a large number of British Foreign Office telegrams of which copies came into German hands. The telegrams never reached Hitler's desk, because his underlings disputed which of them should have the credit of laying them before the Leader. They demonstrated in much detail the mounting power of the allies, especially in the air. It is not quite clear whether their acquisition was a genuine coup by the German secret service, or a daring bluff by their opposite numbers. The Germans paid £300,000 for them—in forged Bank of England notes.

their own inhabitants, who had spent anything up to four years in the local resistance movements. Most of these bodies had looked for support to London, where de Gaulle maintained a free French government, and had been armed by the RAF. They had kept in touch with the free world in various ways, and had done much even before the invasion to keep the occupying armies' nerves on edge; working always in the knowledge that capture meant torture and death. Small parties of British parachutists also caused disproportionately large disorganization behind the German lines, where they could operate with a friendly population.

One drastic attempt was made, in September, to bring Germany down at a blow, by seizing the Rhine crossing at Arnhem in Holland by airborne descent, and penetrating thence into Germany north of the Ruhr; but the attempt just failed of success. So everyone in Europe had to settle down to another winter of war. From June 1944 to March 1945 southern England had to endure a peculiarly savage bombardment. First came pilotless flying bombs with jet engines; then long-range rockets. The rockets were mercifully silent—until they exploded; but they too carried a charge of a ton. With these, with a revolutionary new kind of submarine, and with even more frightful weapons, Hitler hoped to break the nerve of the British; but again he failed. His judgement, always erratic, was slipping; he lived in a remote Polish forest, directing in insane detail those of his generals whom he had not executed after some of them tried to kill him in July 1944.

The Germans held on with a doggedness that belied a remark in *Mein Kampf* that no one will go on fighting when he knows that all is lost : so strong were the double bonds of patriotism and the secret police that they battled on dourly all through the winter on three fronts on land, while their cities were obliterated by American day and RAF night bombers.

The Russians conquered most of Poland in the second half of 1944—waiting for six weeks just outside Warsaw, while the Polish resistance movement in that city, which would have been an embarrassment to the communists, was stamped out by the Germans with their usual severity. Early in 1945 they pressed on into Germany; the Americans and British moved forward also from the west and south; German resistance collapsed at last before an overwhelming weight of metal, and the allied armies met on the Elbe. Hitler shot himself in the flaming ruins of Berlin on 30 April, and the last German armed forces surrendered.

As the allied troops advanced across Germany they overran the concentration camps where the nazis had kept people racially or politically irreconcilable with their regime. The appalling conditions of terror and starvation in which these unhappy people had lived—or, far more often, had died—were thus revealed. Dearly as victory had been bought in lives and effort, the revelation made it clear that it had been right to pay even so high a price.

By the end of the war it had already become clear that the victors were falling out among themselves. They all had one policy towards Hitler—the demand for unconditional surrender. But they were fighting for different goals; and the difference between their goals was confused by a similarity of language. The British and the Americans were each fighting to preserve democracy, and freedom, and peace; and what the two peoples meant by those words was not quite the same. Yet what either of them meant by democracy, freedom, and peace varied little compared with the entirely different meanings attached by the communist government of Russia to the same terms. In the last year of the war it became clear that two sides were forming for a forthcoming struggle for power—the British and Americans on one, the Russians on the other; and that neither side believed the other was sincere.

Negociations were bedevilled for a while by Roosevelt's belief that he could manage Stalin better than Churchill could, and by deep-seated American suspicions of British imperialism. At the three-power conferences held at Teheran (November 1943) and at Yalta (February 1944) there was some tendency on the Americans' part to 'gang up' with the Russians against the British. Roosevelt's English friends noticed at Yalta that his health seemed to be failing; and he died suddenly two months later. He was succeeded in his tremendous office by Harry Truman, the vice-president, who had so far had nothing to do with the strategic direction of the war. Truman soon showed himself a man of intelligence and courage; but he had all the practical business of command to learn.

Churchill had long been suspicious of Russian imperialist intentions, and his suspicions were deepened by the tragedy of Warsaw, and by a civil war in Greece in December 1944. When the Germans evacuated Greece British troops arrived; and the communist-dominated half of the Greek resistance movement tried to seize power. The British were in friendly relations with the exiled Greek king and his government, and intervened sharply to maintain the established order, which Churchill thought the majority of Greeks approved. This intervention, which suppressed the rising, was much criticized in England and America by people who did not perceive communism as a danger: later events may be held to have justified it. Stalin had previously agreed with Churchill that Greece was to lie outside Russia's sphere of influence, so there was no breath of criticism in the communist press; but Churchill could not believe that the Greek communists had attacked Athens without the consent of Moscow.

While the greatest powers were drifting apart in fact, they engaged in an effort to hold together more closely in form. A conference of many nations met at San Francisco in the summer of 1945 and set up the United Nations to replace the League. Its structure followed similar lines, except that the sanctions clauses were more explicit and the unanimity clause was dropped; in its place, the five powers with permanent seats on the security council—America, Russia, Great Britain, France, and China— were to have a right of veto over any motion of substance. This voting compromise had been arranged at Yalta. Few of the golden hopes of the League of Nations Union and the League to Enforce Peace were left at San Francisco; sadder men set up what they trusted was a more viable institution.

Soon after the war with Germany was over, parliament was dissolved—there had been no general election for nearly ten years. Voting took place on 5 July; but the votes were not counted for three weeks. Before the result was known, Churchill and Attlee* had left for a conference at Potsdam, at which the

---

* Attlee was no longer deputy prime minister: the coalition had broken up at the end of May, and Churchill was at the head of an interim conservative government.

victor powers parcelled out Germany into zones of occupation, and Stalin made it clear that the western frontier of Poland had been moved, and was going to stay, much farther west in formerly German territory than his allies at Yalta had realized.

On 25 July the principal British delegates left the conference, to return to London and hear the election result next day—a large labour majority.

CHAPTER X

NO WAR—NO PEACE

1945–1956

CHURCHILL'S unexpected defeat in the election was not a vote of censure on his conduct of the war, for which he had deserved surpassingly well of his country; it was the price he paid for having devoted himself, wholly, for five years, to foreign and military affairs. The electorate remembered the poor record of pre-war conservative governments, and saw that standing up to the dictators, as Baldwin and Chamberlain had been so reluctant to do, had brought the victory at which everybody rejoiced. They looked forward, as well as back. Unconscious of any impending danger from Russia, and conscious of the common share in the sacrifices of the war, they noticed that in the past five years much had been done, in spite of all the difficulties, to look after the wants of ordinary people and establish a more egalitarian society: confidence in state action to promote welfare had been created. Three votes were cast against the conservatives for every two that were cast for them; the labour party had a majority of 148 in the new house of commons. The liberals got over two million votes, but only a dozen seats.

Attlee became prime minister, and formed a cabinet of twenty. After a moment's hesitation, he made a shrewd choice for his foreign secretary—Ernest Bevin. Bevin never pretended to be anything but a plain, blunt working man. Though he was no expert in foreign affairs, he was a highly skilled trade union negociator; he was also a man of immense, sturdy common sense, and great force of character. The Foreign Office staff, who came from very different social strata, took to him at once, and they worked in amicable concord. Bevin put through a reform of the foreign service, prepared under Eden, which was intended to make entry into the service easier for people who had no family connexions attaching them to the aristocracy or the professional class. The reform has not yet produced any marked change.

Attlee went back to Potsdam, taking Bevin with him, for the second half of the conference; but like Churchill and Eden they had to accept the accomplished fact of the Polish frontier. The conservative ministers had contemplated some form of protest; their labour successors, with much new business on their hands, felt unable to make any.

Meanwhile the war with Japan was still going on. It was summarily brought to an end by the Americans. All through the war the four greatest powers had pursued intense research into the possibilities of producing a new explosive, of terrifying power, by splitting the atom. The Germans, fortunately for the British, secured no results; the Russians did little better. By the middle of 1942 both the British and the Americans felt that they were getting near the solution; and agreed to co-operate in trying to make an atomic bomb, in America. The project cost over £400m, and absorbed the finest scientific brains in both countries and in Canada, under a cloak of profound secrecy. Nothing was ready in time to be used against Germany; but soon after the German surrender the dreadful fruit ripened. On 4 July 1945, Churchill records, his caretaker cabinet approved the bomb's use in principle, with 'unanimous, automatic, unquestioned agreement'; all details were left to the Americans.

On 6 August they exploded one of these weapons over the Japanese port of Hiroshima. Over 60,000 people, out of a quarter of a million inhabitants, were killed at once; about 100,000 were injured; practically the whole city vanished in blast and fire. The Russians at once declared war on Japan, to qualify for the status of victor at the coming far eastern peace settlement; and after another atomic explosion at Nagasaki, which inflicted even heavier casualties, the Japanese asked for terms on the fourteenth. None were offered. They signed an instrument of unconditional surrender on 2 September.

The use of the new bomb was defended at the time on the paradoxical ground that it saved lives. Certainly the casualties which would have been incurred on both sides, in the otherwise indispensable invasion of Japan, would have been a great deal—perhaps ten times, perhaps twenty times—more severe. But the argument from casualties seemed more convincing then than it does today, when the sinister genetic implications of the bomb are becoming clearer. And to use the bomb at all appalled millions of people, all over the world, who found it hard to make a moral distinction between such a weapon as this and the barbarities of the concentration camps that had just been destroyed in Germany.

However, the brute facts that the Americans had got the bomb, had used it, and might use it again, dominated the strategy, and hence the diplomacy, of the post-war years. British casualties in the war had been only half as severe as in 1914–18 : about 400,000 dead (60,000 of them in air raids). But the economic losses had been crippling. Emerging from the war £3,000m in debt on their overseas balances, and having no atomic bomb of their own (though they had contributed largely to the Americans' success in making one), the British could do nothing but follow as discreetly as they could in the footsteps of the USA, doing their tactful best to direct American policy away from any obviously dangerous path.

To throw themselves on the mercy of the Russians instead held out little appeal to either great party, or to the public. Some members of the labour party had indeed, during the election campaign, played on the widespread admiration for Russia in Britain, and used the slogan 'left can speak to left'—that is, a British labour government would be able to get on to good terms with a Russian communist one, because both believed in a socialist organization of industry. They forgot that communists as a rule hate socialists more than anybody else. If the socialists are right, then the better organized society that socialists and communists alike are trying to build can be achieved without the violence and the discipline that the communists say are indispensable ; and therefore the whole basis of the communist creed disappears. As it turned out, the labour government got, if anything, rather less respect from the Russians than the coalition had done. Contact with the realities of international affairs while the party was in office convinced all but the incorrigible Russophils in the labour party that hopes of close Anglo-Russian co-operation were illusory, unless at the price of total subjection, which only a communist government would have been ready to pay ; and the communist party had just received derisory support in the election, returning only two members to Westminster. In any case, Russia had been so devastated by the war that for the time being it was out of the question for her to offer economic aid abroad at all.

There was talk for a while of a 'third force', holding the balance between east and west; but it was only talk, based on no realities of power, and must remain so, till either the commonwealth or western Europe is much more integrally bound together, or some truly great power emerges elsewhere.

The Russians were much taken aback by the advent of the atomic bomb. Still confident in their vast army, which they kept largely in being, while the British and the Americans demobilized theirs, they intended to build a big navy, partly equipped with German super-submarines. They provided themselves with a more solid barrier of subject states and provinces to the westward than ever before, reaching far into central Europe: Poland, Hungary, Roumania, Bulgaria, Yugoslavia, Albania had communist-dominated governments, and the Russians had armies of occupation in Austria, and in Germany as far west as Saxony. They hoped to spread communist influence farther yet, through the prestige of their military power. Now suddenly they found their military power was obsolete: in the new field of nuclear physics they were, for a time, left behind.

They applied themselves promptly to the task of catching up, confident enough in their ability to do so to reject a generous American proposal that all nuclear weapons should be prohibited; and they had a big stroke of luck as well. Fuchs, a German refugee physicist of outstanding ability and a British subject, had worked on the first atomic bombs in America, and then came back to England to join the British staff for making them that was set up after the war, when the Americans abruptly ended lend-lease and the three-nation nuclear research team was broken up.

Fuchs was one of those intellectuals who had become convinced, in the thirties, that the only ultimate hope for the world lay in the spread of communism; he was an internationalist, with no loyalty to any particular country; and while he appeared to his colleagues as one of themselves, from time to time he handed over news of what they were doing to the Russians. By mere chance, he happened not to be passing information to the Russians during

L

the periods when he was under routine security investigation. Eventually he could not stand the strain, confessed what he had done, and went to prison; but meanwhile he had explained to the Russians precisely how atomic bombs work, and saved them some years' research.

It is important to remember that he was not a scoundrel, seeking money or notoriety, but a committed man, seeking to do what seemed to him to be right. For his case, and the somewhat comparable ones of Hiss and Maclean, communist agents who rose high in the American and British foreign services before they were found out, show how hard it is in modern international politics to know for certain who is on whose side. Front, flanks, and rear have disappeared from politics as they have from war, and the necessary all-round defences are even harder to establish.

To make atomic bombs seemed necessary even to a labour cabinet, though the labour party was divided on the issue, its pacifist and near-communist wings disapproving for opposite reasons. It was felt by the majority that to abstain from making atomic bombs, when the capacity to make them existed, and when Russia was busy trying to make them too, would be to abdicate without due cause from Britain's position as a great power. General opinion in the country reluctantly concurred.

In the great game of bluff played between the powers after 1945 the Russians sought to manoeuvre themselves into favourable positions without exposing themselves to nuclear devastation before they had their own atomic bombs; the Americans sought to check them, with the bomb as an implied threat in the background; the British, who let the Americans keep some of the bomber bases they had built in England during the war, at first could only watch the game as bystanders. When in March 1950 the Russians got their first atomic bomb, the stakes were raised, but the game went on. The British were more ready to take a hand in it themselves when they produced a bomb of their own in October 1952; but this new card was overtrumped when the Americans and the Russians went on to produce and test, in 1954 and 1955 respectively, thermo-nuclear fission-fusion-fission hydrogen bombs some hundreds of times more powerful still, each producing a crater alone about a mile across.

The British decided to make these also, testing their first in 1957. Both parties approved; the consent of public opinion was less certain, as more and more people came to realize that even a test explosion of a hydrogen bomb kills several hundred human beings at least, nearly all of them as yet unborn.

Against this macabre background, which loomed in states-men's minds as a picture of impending disaster, many events in international politics which before the war would have seemed of the first importance now looked comparatively petty. Firm peace treaties were made with Germany's lesser European allies, including stringent disarmament clauses, since broken without reproof. No reparations payments were exacted; but a fair quantity of machine tools was removed by the victors—to the subsequent advantage of a re-tooled Germany. Italy kept south Tirol, whence a quarter of the Germans had been deported, under Hitler, to Alsace; but she handed her colonies over to the United Nations. One of them, appropriately enough, was given to Ethiopia as a 'trust territory', the new name for a mandate. Austria was re-created, but occupied by the victors' troops till 1955. No treaty was made with ruined Germany; though the British, even more generous than at Vereeniging, provided £80m worth of food for her in the year that followed the war. Germany has allied forces there still, but the ruins have gone, but the occupying troops have become visitors. Yet no one regards the present state of Germany as final; and all attempts to settle it have failed over reluctance to concede the frontier for Poland which Stalin's armies created and Russian refusal to expose the communist-dominated government of the Russian zone of Germany to a free election. In 1952 the three 'western' zones of Germany—American, British, and French—were amalgamated to make one sovereign state; the Russians made their zone into another. It is usually taken for granted that the two states ought to become one again; though the historical case against any such step, based on the menace that a united Germany has usually been to her neighbours, is strong. Much evidence bearing on this point was produced in the trial of nazi leaders before an international court at Nuremberg in the winter of 1945–46. The trial established important points in international law, particularly the illegality of aggressive war and the power of 'natural justice' to override 'superior orders'. Yet it was pervaded with an atmosphere of superior force, for it resulted solely from the allied victory; and the paradox of a Russian sitting in judgement on Germans for using forced labour, an important feature of the Russian home economy, did not escape notice. Ribbentrop was one of the twelve men condemned to death.

The French continued to look with distrust and suspicion on any signs of German revival. To hearten them, the British joined them in 1947 in a fifty-year treaty of mutual military assistance, if either were attacked; it was signed at Dunkirk. The French were more interested at that moment in economic than in military aid. This the British could not provide, for they were wrestling with one of their now frequent crises of indebtedness. But the Americans could; and a British initiative helped them to do so. In June 1947 the American secretary of state, General Marshall, proposed that all Europe should organize itself economically, and offered American help if it did. It was Bevin who called a meeting of all the states of Europe to discuss these proposals; and from this followed the vast Marshall plan for American assistance to European recovery. It was a grandiose project—it had to be, to attract the enthusiasm of the American public; and it was pregnant, as Bevin saw, with future possibilities for a co-operative integration of Europe. Stalin saw these possibilities too, and set his face against the plan. He peremptorily forbade Russia's satellites to take any share in it; he was also able to get Czechoslovakia to withdraw her original application to be included. Czechoslovakia was by now Russia's immediate neighbour; its easternmost province had been annexed by Russia in 1945. In February 1948 the Czech communist party seized power in Prague, by a neatly planned *coup d'état*, and the country was added to the satellite group.

In June Yugoslavia, hitherto an obedient satellite in appearance, though in reality recalcitrant, broke away from the Stalinist bloc, and Stalin in his turn could take no action. In the following winter he tried to isolate the western sectors of Berlin from road and rail contact with the rest of the world (Berlin lay well inside the Russian zone of Germany); but the American and British air forces defeated this attempt by flying supplies over the top of the blockade, and in the spring Stalin desisted.

By this time the Russian government made no secret of the hostility it felt for the British and Americans, and had made plentiful use, to their harm, of its United Nations veto power. In face of this threat, Bevin turned to counter-measures. In March 1948 he secured the Brussels treaty, by which five states —Britain, France, Belgium, Holland, and Luxemburg—all agreed to give each other help if any of them were attacked. Bevin and Acheson (who succeeded Marshall as American secretary of state at the end of the year) then pressed on with a wider scheme, the North Atlantic treaty organization (NATO). By this treaty, signed in April 1949, ten western European nations* joined the USA and Canada in declaring 'that an armed attack against one or more of them in Europe or North America shall be considered an attack against them all', and would bring with it armed action by all of them against the attacking power. This was a regional arrangement for collective security within the general framework of the United Nations system.

The Brussels treaty and NATO were intended to be military counterparts of the Marshall plan, steps towards the closer integration of the states of Europe, weak by themselves, whose united strength would be respectable. NATO's founding treaty arranged for a defence committee of its members to be set up at once, to review and prepare plans for military action; and much detailed work by staff officers of member countries has been done since.

It has turned out impossible to separate military, political, and economic measures to promote that closer European union for which Bevin and Churchill, in their different ways, were both pressing in the late forties. On the economic side, six countries— Belgium, France, Holland, Italy, Luxemburg, and western Germany—agreed in 1951 to pool their coal and steel resources in a European Coal and Steel Community (ECSC). The British hesitated whether to join ECSC; in the end they stayed outside

---

* Belgium, Denmark, France, Holland, Iceland, Italy, Luxemburg, Norway, Portugal, and the United Kingdom. Greece, Turkey, and western Germany have since joined. Ireland, it will be noticed, does not belong.

it. This was partly for the economic reason that the British coal and steel industries serve different markets from the continental ones, partly for the political reason that the ECSC takes its decisions by majority vote, no member having a veto—so decisions disagreeable to either side of the industries in the United Kingdom might be forced upon them if they joined.

Lurking behind this political reason was a bigger one, which in various ways affected all the governments of Europe west of the Russian-dominated bloc: all were, and are, unwilling to surrender any part of their national sovereignty to any supranational organization, though in many of them public opinion would strongly favour some form of 'Western Union'. That is why the various political projects for unifying Europe have lagged. It may yet turn out that the effect of such bodies as the ECSC, or the Benelux customs union of Belgium, Holland, and Luxemburg, will be to promote unification without attracting the notice of the politicians till their reluctance to unite has dwindled.

Though the affairs of Europe must always be of vital concern to the United Kingdom, the existence of the British commonwealth and the extent of British trading interests overseas make it impossible for British governments to fail to look outside Europe as well. Between 1945 and 1951, while Attlee was prime minister, fundamental changes were made in the structure of the commonwealth, in conformity with long-established labour party policy.

This policy was based on an appreciation of the new national problems that have recently grown up, almost all of them among peoples who are not of European stock, who insist that they have a natural right to govern themselves after their own fashion, in entire independence of any foreign supervisors. Tact, sympathy, and intelligent administration, combined with an ultimate readiness to concede self-government, subject to certain strategic safeguards, will now no longer suffice to meet demands that have become more and more categorical since the war.

The labour party, like the liberal party before it, had been interested for years in letting India govern itself, as soon as it was fit to do so; during the war Attlee and Cripps had forced the cabinet to declare in principle that India was to have self-government after it. But the Indians showed little sign of coming to any agreement among themselves, and the extremist parties in India accused the British of fostering Indian dissensions in order to retain their own power, on the old principle of *divide et impera*. So in February 1947 Attlee, by the most considerable act of statesmanship of his life, announced that the British would in any case relinquish their authority in India within eighteen months. He thus imposed practical responsibilities on the Indian leaders. Religious rivalries proving insuperable, they had to agree among themselves to divide their country in two ; in August Hindu India and Moslem Pakistan both became dominions, fully independent of control from London. Both subsequently proclaimed themselves republics, though remaining 'associated' with the British commonwealth, of which the only formal link is the crown. Many conservatives grumbled at this settlement ; Churchill was particularly hostile to it. He remembered India as he had seen it as a hussar subaltern in the nineties ; he did not believe the Indians were fit to govern themselves, or would soon be ; he had long struggled against those in his own party who thought they were. The labour party, however, strongly supported Indian independence, and the British public on the whole agreed that it was not reasonable to try to hold India against the will of its inhabitants, which seemed clearly enough expressed in favour of self-government. The price was high—something like half a million Indians killed in racial and religious riots in the second half of 1947; but it was generally thought worth paying.

Attlee's government applied similar policies in several other places. Ceylon became a dominion. Burma became entirely independent; so did southern Ireland. Big strides towards self-government were made in Jamaica and in the west African colonies of Nigeria and the Gold Coast. In the Levant, the mandates over Palestine and Transjordan were given up, and the new states of Israel and Jordan recognized. The surrounding Arab states went to war with Israel, with singularly little success. But the most populous of them, Egypt, succeeded in spite of its military weakness in pursuing a policy of such resolute intransigence towards the British that they at last agreed to withdraw all their troops and installations from the Suez canal zone, and from the Sudan, which for over fifty years had been under joint Anglo-Egyptian administration and has now just attained independence.

The war had proved that the Mediterranean route was not, after all, indispensable to imperial defence; so some strategic justification could be provided for leaving the canal zone. The real keystone of the arch of imperial strategy seems to be Cape Town; and the consequent need for amicable relations with the Union of South Africa, in spite of the South African policy of *apartheid* that seems detestable to most British people, has had unfortunate effects on British policies in central Africa.

Elsewhere the policy of colonial concession has not always had satisfactory results. The troubles in Cyprus current in 1956 are a direct result of the decision to leave the canal zone, since it is held strategically undesirable to leave the Levant with no British base in it at all, a vacuum into which Russia would undoubtedly move. Some colonial populations have been encouraged, by the news of concessions granted elsewhere, to demand more for themselves than the British have thought them ready to receive; and substantial British forces have had to be used in recent years both to deal with a savage revolt in Kenya and to hold down British Guiana, and above all Malaya.

The new problems of eastern Asia have indeed proved as dangerous as the old problems of Europe to the British in the past ten years; British opinion has been much less fully informed about them, and for lack of information has inevitably found it hard to enter into full sympathy with the aspirations of many eastern Asian peoples that were awakened during the war. Meanwhile, there are still British interests in Asia that need to be amicably liquidated, and others that it is felt necessary to try to preserve.

Two events in the far east have been of cardinal importance for British foreign policy. Firstly, the communist party of China, which had long had its own army, and kept some provinces under its own control after it fell out with Chiang Kai-shek's nationalist government in 1941, succeeded in conquering mainland China in 1949. Chiang retired to Formosa, where he still maintains what he and the Americans regard as the legitimate government of China, which has a power of veto in the United Nations security council; but the communists have meanwhile established their hold firmly over six hundred million people, and are trying simultaneously to extend their frontiers and to carry through an industrial revolution.

Chinese communism has always differed from Russian, for it has based itself on the peasantry, not on the urban proletariat; Stalin had an acrid quarrel with Mao Tse-tung in the twenties, in which he denied that this could be done. In 1949 Mao proved him wrong, and is now prime minister of China. But no other ally than Russia was available to the new Chinese state; and in February 1950 the two powers signed a thirty-year alliance. This created a considerable shift in the world balance of power. The British (unlike the Americans) early gave *de facto* recognition to the new Chinese government, but relations between Britain and China were far from cordial, and the Chinese proceeded to evict the long-established British merchants from China altogether.

The second critical event was the war in Korea. On 25 June 1950 fighting broke out along the 38th parallel of latitude, the artificial frontier which had divided Korea since the end of the war, when the Russians took the north and the Americans took the south part of the peninsula under their protection. North and south Koreans each accused the other of provoking the conflict. Possibly both were right; but as the north Koreans had already mobilized, and the south Koreans had not, it seems that the north Koreans had wider ambitions than mere local trouble-making, and were seeking to conquer the whole country at once. The fighting was immediately brought to the attention of the security council, where by a curious accident no Russian delegate happened to be present. The security council declared that north Korea had committed an act of aggression, and the enforcement provisions of the charter were shortly put in action against it. American troops were in fact already on their way to the Korean front from Japan.

This first collective security war vindicated the United Nations organization in principle, and showed that it was worthy of some trust by small states threatened with aggression. Seventeen nations, including the British and three dominions, sent troops to fight under the United Nations' flag; though the Americans, who alone incurred heavy casualties among the intervening powers, provided the strategic command and the bulk of the troops. But the vindication was partial, not complete. One of the security council's permanent members, Russia, consistently supported with equipment and advice the communist government of the side that had been declared in the wrong. China, alarmed for her Manchurian frontier when the Americans began to advance north of the 38th parallel in the autumn, sent a large army of 'volunteers' to fight on the northern side. She was herself, as a result, denounced as an aggressor by the United Nations assembly in February 1951; but incurred no sanctions in consequence. Moreover the United Nations troops in Korea could have little respect for the regime they had been sent to defend; and United Nations opinion was for some time troubled by Chinese allegations that the Americans were using germ warfare. These allegations at first appeared well founded; they were eventually shewn to be baseless. The fortunes of the war varied; over three years passed before it was brought to an uneasy close, with the two halves of Korea devastated, but politically much as they had been before it began, and everybody concerned disillusioned and out of temper.

The outbreak of war in Korea seemed in western Europe to be a sign that the communists, now that Russia too had atomic weapons, were ready to take more risks, and might start a major war. All the NATO countries, led by the British, set about increasing their production of arms. The lesson of the thirties, when western lack of arms had made it possible for Hitler and Mussolini to attain positions of such strength that they had to be fought on the widest scale, weighed heavily on the consciences of statesmen and planners, who were determined at least not to make that mistake again. But the cost in economic dislocation was severe.

The labour government's main interest had been in home affairs; it had been elected on a programme of nationalization and 'fair shares', and carried much of it out. Some basic industries and services were brought under state control, and the welfare services which had been begun during the war were extended. At

a general election in February 1950* foreign affairs played little
part in the campaign, except for a suggestion of Churchill's that
the new prime minister, whoever he might be, should go and talk
to Stalin about atomic energy (the Americans had just announced
that work had begun on a hydrogen bomb). Bevin promptly
characterized this as a 'stunt proposal'. There was a particularly
heavy poll (84%), and the result was practically a draw, the
labour party being left in office with a barely perceptible majority
of half-a-dozen. This meant that another election would have to
be fought before long, so electioneering was endemic at Westminster till it took place eighteen months later : this made both
parties particularly tentative in all their policies.

In the following winter Bevin's health broke down, and he
resigned in March 1951. Herbert Morrison succeeded him;
he was also a man of humble origins, the son of a London police-
man, who had risen through the municipal labour party in
London's local government, and served as home secretary in
Churchill's coalition. His nimble mind and negociating skill
were useful at the Foreign Office, but he came comparatively
unprepared to foreign affairs, and lacked Bevin's extraordinary
strength of character.

Morrison was soon plunged into a tangled dispute in the
middle east. The Persians suddenly nationalized, without compensation, the plant and refinery at Abadan on the Persian Gulf
of the Anglo-Iranian oil company, in which the British government held 51% of the shares. They had no legal right to do so,
but disregarded protests from the international court, and
'dared' the British to use force against them. This the British were
afraid to do, because Russia lay at the other end of Persia from
Abadan, and might well seize on her claim (under an alliance
with Persia of 1921) to join in any fighting, on Persia's side :
strong British action against Persia might, in fact, unleash a great
war, in which it would be easy for the Russians to paint the
British as old-fashioned imperialist aggressors, and difficult for
the Americans to come in on the British side.

* Iti s an illuminating sidelight on the Russian attitude to the British
at the time that Moscow wireless station informed its home listeners about
what went on at a British general election by broadcasting extracts from the
Pickwick Papers.

So the British fell back on an inglorious withdrawal from Abadan. It was very unlike what Lord Palmerston would have done; but Lord Palmerston's days were over. Given the labour government's premises about the importance of preserving peace and about the immorality of 'colonialism', and the awe-inspiring risks attending on ferocity, however just ferocity might be, there was nothing else to do. But what was done, was done slowly and with an ill grace. The British lost heavily in prestige abroad; and the labour government lost in popularity at home.

A general election followed at once, in October 1951. There was again a large poll (over 82%); and the labour party made what it could of the charge that the conservatives were warmongers. It managed both to increase its own poll and to get more votes than the conservatives; but it lost the election. Many more liberal voters turned right than turned left; the liberal vote came down well below a million, and only six liberal MPs got back to parliament. The new house of commons had a small but workable conservative majority; Churchill, at seventy-five, once more became prime minister, and Eden returned to the Foreign Office.

They devoted their main attention to a plan for a European defence community (EDC) which the Americans were urging on Europe. This was to be a supra-national body with control over the armies of the ECSC countries—including western Germany. The arguments from recent history against rearming Germany at all were of exceptional strength: German militarism had ranked high among the underlying causes of war in 1914, and the German rearmament programme of 1935 had been a prime cause of war in 1939. Yet though it seemed as if her neighbours dared not allow Germany to arm herself once more, it also seemed as if they dared not fail to do so. They discounted German claims for 'equality of rights'; but they were impressed with the danger from the east. The Russians were, and are, believed to have about $3\frac{1}{2}$m ground troops available for deployment, at short notice, into western Europe: and all the general staffs said that without a German field force, well forward in the presumable battle zone, the red armies could not be stopped from cutting straight through to the

Atlantic. The danger indeed seemed so acute that, in the face of it, even the recent iniquities of the German concentration camps had to be set aside. The EDC plan proposed the formation of small bodies of German troops, so closely integrated into a common European army that there could be no danger of re-creating a German military menace to the rest of Europe; and Germany was not to manufacture atomic, bacteriological, or chemical weapons. This would, it was hoped, provide the necessary man-power to place in the way of communist armies, without producing a Frankenstein's monster that would be able to get out of its creator's control.

The British government was tempted by the idea of joining EDC. (The public found the subject altogether too complicated, and had no formed opinion.) If the British stayed out, the French and the Germans would be left as the only countries of any real weight in the community, for Italy was both economically weak and not far from revolution at home, and the Benelux countries were small; and the French had an uneasy feeling that they might before long find themselves overshadowed by the Germans, unless they had the British standing by their side. They had little trust in the effectiveness of paper fetters. On the other hand, if the British came in, what—familiar cry—was to be done about commonwealth and imperial obligations? By an ingenious compromise, the government announced in April 1952 that the British would be 'associated' with EDC; without actually belonging to it, British forces would work closely with the new European army, and assimilate weapons and tactics to those of the community. Next month the EDC treaty, an elaborate document of 131 articles and many appendices, was signed. In many ways its institutions were linked with ECSC; the two agreements, in fact, were complementary.

Though the treaty had been signed, it had yet to be ratified; and most French politicians still doubted whether the new arrangements were really to France's advantage. Over and over again the essential ratification debate was put off; and when at last the vote was taken (30 August 1954) the treaty was rejected by 319 to 264, and the whole structure fell to the ground.

Much had happened meanwhile. The American presidential election in November 1952 had been won by Churchill's friend

General Eisenhower, supreme commander in France during the war, by a record majority; but the party to which he adhered, the republicans, secured only a narrow majority in congress from the democrats. Dulles, who as a young man had been one of Wilson's 'experts' at Paris, was the new American secretary of state; no master of tact, he terrified Europeans by a reference in January 1954 to the 'massive and instant retaliatory power' which atomic bombs gave the USA. This was a move in the old game of bluff and counter-bluff, which he played with vigour, seeking to 'contain' the communists within their frontiers by threats of annihilation if they moved beyond them, and not hesitating to go to the brink of war.

Communist policy had also undergone some variation. Stalin died in March 1953; and the question of who was to succeed him in control remained for some time obscure. On 17 June that year there were widespread risings in eastern Germany, the revolt of an urban proletariat maddened beyond endurance by the conditions under which the ruling communist minority made it live. The risings were put down easily enough by Russian troops, acting with speed and brutality worthy of the Gestapo; but that they had taken place at all was fatal to Beria, the head of the Russian security police and one of the competitors for Stalin's place: appropriately enough, he suffered in December the judicial murder he had meted out to so many himself.

The Russians of course opposed EDC with all the resources of propaganda, intrigue, and misrepresentation at their command, and denounced the western powers for suggesting that western Germany should be rearmed. This was mere doubletalk: they had already set up an army nearly 100,000 strong in eastern Germany, called 'police', but equipped with aircraft, tanks, and artillery.

When the French eventually refused to ratify EDC, Eden made full use of his charm and negociating skill—great qualifications for his post—to persuade the EDC countries to arrive at agreements which re-established the community in a somewhat different form. Under these agreements, signed in London and Paris in October 1954, there was to be a German army of twelve divisions, tied as firmly as is possible on paper to the NATO powers. So distant did the war already seem that Germany and Italy were invited to join the Brussels treaty also. The British promised to keep four divisions and a tactical air force on the continent indefinitely, unless some imperial emergency forced their withdrawal. The occupation of western Germany was formally ended; in return, the Germans invited their late British, American, and French conquerors to keep troops there.

All this was done, rapidly but efficiently, in spite of the new Russian approach to problems of foreign policy that followed Stalin's death. This new approach has so far been almost entirely one of form and not of substance: the Russians have been bon-homous and cheerful instead of surly and carping, but their aims remain the same. One actual concession has been made by them: they have withdrawn their forces of occupation from Austria, which has again become entirely independent. They have not yet consequently withdrawn, as they legally should have done, the troops with which they buttress the puppet governments of Hungary and Roumania. Their smiles have been so winning that many ordinary people in the west have been tempted to drop their guard; but the men responsible for policy-making in all the western countries have been bitten so often by the Russians that they are made more suspicious, not less, by the appearance of amicability. The Russians' tactics have so far succeeded in influencing public opinion in the west as to suggest that devastat-ing results might have been achieved had Stalin adopted them in 1945; but they did not suit a character crabbed by long years in the revolutionary underground of tsarist days. Now it would seem they have been adopted too late for use in Europe or America, though they may yet achieve important results in Asia.

The main effect of the Russians' amiable manners on the west, so far, has been to foster the delusion that a meeting between the effective heads of the great powers will, of itself, smooth away all major stumbling-blocks in international relations. This ignores the lesson of diplomatic history that the most successful confer-ences are those at which what is to be decided has been arranged beforehand through the normal channels of diplomacy. Only one other kind of conference is likely to do useful business: that at which one of the parties arrives prepared to surrender. It was a conference of this second kind, a meeting of foreign ministers at Geneva, that secured in July 1954 a patched-up peace in

Indo-China, where France had been fighting a hopeless battle for years. Eden, with charm and dexterity, managed to persuade the French to admit their defeat; it was done so gracefully that it almost looked like a victory. Another possible source of a major war was thus, for a time at any rate, removed; and Eden's prestige rose accordingly. The British agreed to join a South-east Asia Treaty Organization (SEATO) established by the Americans that September; Australia, France, New Zealand, Pakistan, the Philippines, and Siam were the other members; its terms were similar to those of NATO.

In April 1955 Churchill finally decided that he was too old for active politics, and resigned. Eden succeeded him, and dissolved parliament next month. Fewer people voted than in 1950 or 1951 (there was a 77% poll); and though the conservative vote fell by over a million, the labour vote fell by a million and a half, and the conservatives increased their majority from a bare 17 to a useful 60. The new foreign secretary, Macmillan, was an experienced parliamentarian; as he had been minister of defence since August 1954, recent foreign affairs were not an entirely fresh subject to him.

At last, in July 1955, the conference 'at the summit' took place at Geneva. Eisenhower and Dulles; Eden and Macmillan; and the current French prime and foreign ministers, Faure and Pinay, represented the western powers. The Russians sent Bulganin, a political soldier, their prime minister; Molotov, foreign minister since May 1939, the last 'old bolshevik' to survive in high office;* and Khrushchov, the party secretary, who seems to have succeeded Stalin as 'No. 1' if anybody has done so. Both sides took a serious view of future prospects if ever hydrogen bombs were dropped in earnest. Macmillan put the conclusion tersely, if inelegantly, when he returned to England: 'There ain't gonna be no war.' But nobody gave any definite undertaking not to use hydrogen bombs; on various telling if minor points, such as allowing more visas for tourists or stopping the jamming of western broadcasts, the Russians maintained their old attitudes with complete intransigence, if with better manners;† and

---

* He and Stalin had edited *Pravda* in 1917.

† On both these points they relented somewhat, as far as the British alone were concerned, when Bulganin and Khrushchov visited England in April 1956.

having talked much, as usual, of 'peace', within a few months of the conference they carried out a test explosion with a particularly large hydrogen bomb. The agreed statement issued at the end of the conference was blunted by a familiar difficulty of language: words and phrases, 'secure peace', 'legitimate interests', 'collective self-defence', meant different things to different sides. The statement took the form of a directive to the four powers' foreign ministers, who met again at Geneva in the autumn, and achieved —as might have been expected—nothing at all.

Eden was less successful in charge of a government than in charge of the Foreign Office. Butler, his principal assistant, was worn out by four years at the exchequer; in December 1955 he was replaced there by Macmillan, who had had no time to make much mark on foreign policy. The new foreign secretary, Selwyn Lloyd, was a lawyer in his early fifties, who had entered the army a private in 1939 and risen to the rank of brigadier by his abilities as a staff officer; like Grey, he spoke no foreign languages well. Had Eden wanted a strong foreign secretary, he had not far to look: his own former deputy Cranborne (Lord Salisbury since 1947) was the ablest member of the cabinet. Any disadvantage that attached to Salisbury's membership of the house of lords could easily have been—but was not—removed by an act of parliament. A more weighty objection to him was that he had acquired a bad reputation among the political public. As an opponent of the Munich settlement, and a man without business interests, he was somewhat out of touch with important elements in his own party; as a strong conservative and an even stronger imperialist, he was anathema to most labour politicians. In any case, he was not made foreign secretary. Eden appointed Lloyd, apparently as a subordinate to do the work of the office and to follow his prime minister's instructions on main lines of policy.

So much had the Arab countries of the near and middle east lost their former respect for the British that before Lloyd had been three months in office a mob stoned the motor-cars that accompanied him through the oil port of Bahrein, during a tour intended to make him more familiar with the problems of those regions. The basic difficulties were these: the enmity between Israel and her Arab neighbours; the anxiety of the British to go

M

on drawing oil from the area, complicated by the temptation to the new Arab states to follow Persia's example and take over their oil resources for themselves; the reluctance of the USA to support any British move that seemed 'imperialistic'; the absence of any firm base from which the British could if need be exert force; and the threat of Russian penetration into an area of particular importance for imperial communications.

Iraq, Persia, Pakistan, and Turkey were grouped by the British into another 'regional organization', the Baghdad pact, early in 1955; an attempt later in the year to persuade Jordan also to enter it encountered a series of rebuffs, culminating in the unceremonious dismissal in March 1956 of the British general who had long led and trained the Jordanian army. The Baghdad pact was much resented by Egypt, the local leader of the Arab countries; and in the autumn of 1955 the delicate balance of forces in the Levant which had been supervised informally for some years by the British, the Americans, and the French was disturbed by a fresh incursion into this field of activity by Russia. The balance had largely been maintained by restrictions on the supply of arms: the Russians upset it by offering arms from their satellite factories, which the Egyptians eagerly accepted —they had no memories of Russia as a 'colonialist' power to deter them, and indeed no political conditions were attached to the deal.

At the time of writing, the situation in the near and middle east remains dangerously near explosion point. Indeed, while these pages are in the press, a sharp crisis has broken out there; for Egypt, following Persia's example, has announced the nationalization of the Suez Canal; and British opinion is ill-informed about it.

Public opinion in the west has been further confused, as the Russians have all along meant it to be, by their appearance of sweet reasonableness, cloaking their usual adamantine inflexibility. As time goes on, the 'Geneva spirit' of which there was so much talk in the press can be seen to mean very little. Khrushchov, however affable, has revealed himself to be a man without regard for the truth: as witness his statement in Bombay in November 1955 that the British, the French, and the Americans had 'started' the second world war by sending the troops of Hitlerite Germany against Russia, contrasted with his attack on Stalin, in Moscow in February 1956, for having neglected Churchill's warnings that Hitler was going to attack him.

Such are the latest opponents of a Great Britain which is no longer among the giant powers, and whose principal remaining strength lies in the moderation and good sense of its electors, who ultimately decide its policy. The Russians' opposition is made more interesting by the serious efforts they are making to introduce some scope for liberality in the regimes they control, and more formidable by their possession of an annihilating weapon against which the British have not yet got ready even the dubious reply of counter-annihilation in return. It is complicated by their tacit entente with some of the Arab countries that hate the British most deeply. The lines of great warships, stretching out of sight in both directions, that dominated the world at Queen Victoria's diamond jubilee review are out of sight indeed.

The British isles, small and densely populated, are peculiarly vulnerable to hydrogen bombs: economic chaos, followed by starvation, could be induced by less than a dozen of them, and no certain means of preventing their arrival is known. The preservation of peace between the great powers, for long the principal interest of British foreign policy, has become of singular importance in the light of this latest development, and not for the British alone. If the third great war of the century, involving the greatest powers with all their greatest weapons, broke out now, the amount of radio-activity released would be so great that in a thousand years' time there would very probably be no life of any kind at all left on the earth. In fact, the stakes in the great game have now been raised so high that no one can play at the highest board any more without staking everything he has. But the danger remains that lack of a full appreciation of consequences, or mere inadvertence, may yet bring on an all-out war.

What the two giants of the modern world and the half-dozen or so of other states with some present title to greatness really dispute about is the oldest question in politics: who is to be master? Part of the trouble between the two camps into which they are divided lies in the conviction of the leaders on each side that they are right, and their enemies are utterly wrong; more, in the strength of the ancient tradition that conflicts of interests between rivals have got, in the end, to be settled by force. Most of all it lies in the state of mind that (to go no farther back) prevented disarmament in the twenties, and ruined the League of Nations in the thirties : mistrust among the peoples. Let us take the central case. No sensible British or American voter can seriously advocate the use of British or American arms to over-throw the Russian regime ; but no sensible British or American voter, looking at the doctrines on which the Russian regime is founded, can fail to fear that the Russians may want to over-throw the regime under which he lives himself. The western peoples, fully conscious that they will not attack, only desire to be armed because they fear an attack from the east. Whether the Russians only desire to be armed because they fear attack from the west, or are determined to carry through one day 'the forcible overthrow of all existing social conditions' in the west that Marx advocated in the communist manifesto, nobody in the west can say. And everybody, easterner, westerner, and neutralist alike, is reluctant to admit the newest answer in politics : that war, great war, has ceased to be an efficient means of carrying on a policy, because it is bound to end in catastrophe.

NOTE ON BOOKS

It may perhaps be of use to pick out, from the multitude of books bearing on recent history, those which have been of particular use to the present writer. His indebtedness to their authors and editors will be apparent. Much fuller reading lists for parts of the period covered will be found in A. L. C. Bullock and A. J. P. Taylor *A select list of books on European history 1815–1914* (Oxford 1949) and in G. P. Gooch *Bibliography of European history 1918–1939* (London 1940: all books are published in London unless otherwise stated).

1. DOCUMENTS.

H. W. V. Temperley and L. M. Penson *Foundations of British foreign policy* (Cambridge 1938) runs from 1792 to 1902, with a penetrating commentary. J. B. Joll *Britain and Europe* (1950) covers a wider range, 1793–1940, on a smaller scale. Gooch and Temperley *British documents on the origins of the war* (13v, 1926–38) cover 1898–1914 in massive detail. There is little useful documentation on either war. E.Ll. Woodward, R.d'O. Butler, and J. P. T. Bury *Documents on British foreign policy 1919–1939* (in progress) is already even longer than Gooch and Temperley, though less informative. A. B. Keith *Speeches and documents on international affairs 1918–1937* (2v, 1938) is useful.

2. HISTORIES AND MONOGRAPHS.

A. J. Grant and Temperley *Europe in the xix and xx centuries* (6 ed, 1952, by Penson), a factual summary; R. W. Seton-Watson *Britain in Europe 1789–1914* (Cambridge 1937); Taylor *The struggle for mastery in Europe 1848–1918* (Oxford 1954); A. J. Marder *British naval policy 1880–1905* (1941). L. Albertini *The Origins of the war of 1914* (1942, translation, 3v, Oxford 1952–56) is ponderously complete on the diplomatic side; it should be read with T. Wolff *The Eve of 1914* (trans. 1935).

C. R. M. F. Cruttwell's is the best *History of the great war* (Oxford 1936). Temperley's *History of the Peace conference of Paris* (6v, 1920–24), a necessary source book, also covers the end of the war. J. M. Keynes *Economic consequences of the Peace* (1919) and *A revision of the treaty* (1922) are indispensable, and his *Two memoirs* (1949) are interesting.

M. Baumont *La Faillite de la paix* (Paris 1945) and G. M. Gathorne-Hardy *Short history of international affairs 1920–39* (4 ed, 1950) are workmanlike and full. F. P. Walters *A history of the League of Nations* (2v, 1952) covers the same period as Gathorne-Hardy with more insight. Among many informative books by J. W. Wheeler-Bennett, *Disarmament and security since Locarno* (1932) and *Munich* (1948) may be singled out. M. Oakeshott *Social and political doctrines of contemporary Europe* (Cambridge 1939) is useful. L. B. Namier *Diplomatic prelude* (1948), supplemented by his two books of essays, *Europe in decay* (1950) and *In the nazi era* (1953), deals with the appeasers in the closing months of peace. F. Borkenau *The communist international* (1938) covers 1917–37.

On British, rather than general European, history, R. C. K. Ensor *England 1870–1914* (Oxford 1936) and C. L. Mowat *Britain between the wars 1918–1940* (1955) have plenty of detail; W. N. Medlicott *British foreign policy since Versailles* (1940) is full; P. A. Reynolds *British foreign policy in the inter-war years* (1954) is analytical; R. W. Seton-Watson *Britain and the Dictators* (Cambridge 1938) and *From Munich to Danzig* (1939) are models of scholarly invective; R. Bassett *Democracy and foreign policy* (1952) is a case history of the Manchurian dispute; in *The history of 'The Times'*, vol. III (1947) covers 1884–1912 and vol. IV (1952) runs from 1912 to 1941. C. Wilmot *Struggle for Europe* (1952) on the second half of the late war; M. A. Fitzsimons *The foreign policy of the British Labour government 1945–1951* (Notre Dame 1953); J. Hampden Jackson *The postwar decade* (1955); *The Economist* (weekly), *passim*.

3. MEMOIRS AND BIOGRAPHIES

J. L. Garvin and J. Amery *Joseph Chamberlain* (4v, 1932–51, unfinished); Newton *Lansdowne* (Macmillan 1929); J. L. Hammond *C. P. Scott* (1934); Grey *Twenty-five years* (2v, 1925); H. Nicolson *Lord Carnock* (1930), a life of his father Arthur Nicolson, *Peacemaking 1919* (1933), and *Curzon: the last phase 1919–25* (1934); D. L. George *War memoirs* (6v, 1933–36) and *The Truth about the peace treaties* (1938); W. S. Churchill *The world crisis 1911–23* (6v, 1923–29) and *The second world war* (6v, 1948–54); M. A. Hamilton *Henderson* (1938); C. Petrie *A. Chamberlain* (2v, 1939 & 1940); K. G. Feiling *N. Chamberlain* (1946); Cecil *A great experiment* (1941); and Templewood (Hoare) *Nine troubled years* (1954).

Outside Great Britain, Bullock *Hitler* (1952); G. Ciano *Diary 1937–43* (2v, 1951 and 1947) and *Diplomatic papers* (ed. M. Muggeridge, 1948); and I. Deutscher *Stalin* (1949). The proceedings of the Nuremberg trial (22v, 1946–51) are depressing, but important.

GOVERNMENTS AND FOREIGN SECRETARIES

date	'the committee of two'		party tone of government
	prime minister	foreign secretary	
June 1895	Salisbury	Salisbury	unionist
Nov. 1900	Salisbury	Lansdowne	unionist
July 1902	Balfour	Lansdowne	unionist
Dec. 1905	Campbell-Bannerman	Grey	liberal
Apr. 1908	Asquith	Grey	liberal
May 1915	Asquith	Grey	liberal & conservative
Dec. 1916	Lloyd George	Balfour	conservative & liberal
Dec. 1918	Lloyd George	Balfour	conservative-dominated
Oct. 1919	Lloyd George	Curzon	conservative-dominated
Oct. 1922	Bonar Law	Curzon	conservative
May 1923	Baldwin	Curzon	conservative
Jan. 1924	MacDonald	MacDonald	labour
Nov. 1924	Baldwin	A. Chamberlain	conservative
May 1929	MacDonald	Henderson	labour
Aug. 1931	MacDonald	Reading	conservative-dominated
Nov. 1931	MacDonald	Simon	conservative-dominated
June 1935	Baldwin	Hoare	conservative
Dec. 1935	Baldwin	Eden	conservative
May 1937	N. Chamberlain	Eden	conservative
Mar. 1938	N. Chamberlain	Halifax	conservative
May 1940	Churchill	Halifax	conservative & labour
Dec. 1940	Churchill	Eden	conservative & labour
May 1945	Churchill	Eden	conservative
July 1945	Attlee	Bevin	labour
Mar. 1951	Attlee	Morrison	labour
Oct. 1951	Churchill	Eden	conservative
Apr. 1955	Eden	Macmillan	conservative
Dec. 1955	Eden	Lloyd	conservative

INDEX

184